THE BOATING
Companion

All You Need to Know for Life on the Water

© 2008 by Quid Publishing
First published in the United States in 2008 by Running Press
Book Publishers

9 8 7 6 5 4 3 2 1
Digit on the right indicates the number of this printing

Library of Congress Control Number: 2007935056

ISBN: 978-0-7624-3186-1

Conceived, designed, and produced by
Quid Publishing
Level 4, Sheridan House, 114 Western Road,
Hove, BN3 1DD
England
www.quidpublishing.com

This book may be ordered by mail from the publisher.
Please include $2.50 for postage and handling.
But try your bookstore first!

Running Press Book Publishers
125 South Twenty-Second Street
Philadelphia, Pennsylvania 19103-4399

Visit us on the web!
www.runningpress.com

Acknowledgments:
Thanks to Alison Bowker for additional research.

THE BOATING Companion

All You Need to Know for Life on the Water

by Rob Beattie

Running Press
Philadelphia • London

Contents

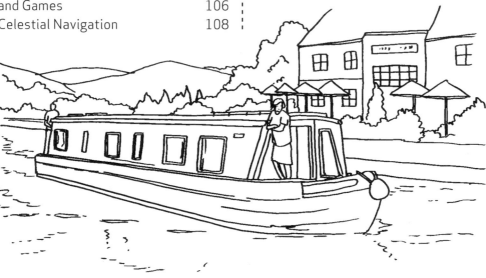

Introduction

It's evening as we sit here, enjoying the last of the early summer sun as it washes the sky white and blue. As always when we're on board, the world is never still—at least, our little bit of it isn't—but rises and falls ever so slightly; it's restful and soothing. A light goes on in the cabin of the boat next door, and there's the sound of low voices. It's been another fine day afloat and frankly, dear reader, we're pleasantly pooped.

A Taste of Freedom

Let's start as we mean to go on. "That's what a ship is, you know," offers Captain Jack Sparrow drunkenly in *Pirates of the Caribbean: The Curse of the Black Pearl.* "It's not just a keel and a hull and a deck and sails; that's what a ship needs. But what a ship is . . . is freedom." While it's unlikely that any of us will share Captain Jack's taste in facial hair, we can definitely share his sentiments, rum-soaked though they may be. A boat—any kind of boat—is, indeed, freedom.

This book aims to give you a taste of that freedom. Whatever your interest and regardless of your level of experience or involvement, the contents are designed to open the door to the worlds of boats and boating, of sailors and sailing, of canoeists and their solitary expeditions into the wild, of canal-boat enthusiasts in their floating living rooms, of laughing kids getting soaked in dinghies, of Mom and Dad still exploring in their senior years, of ancient boats with cracked paint, or new ones not yet named—a peek into the life afloat, a glimpse of what lies beyond the mooring post or harbor wall.

An Activity for Everyone

Boating used to be something of an exclusive club, but these days anyone can afford to be involved in some way, whether it's a couple of hours' boat hire at a local lake, a week's cruising, or a proper sailboat that you care for and sail lovingly most weekends. As long as you are sensible and aware of the potential problems, there are no real age limits when it comes to boating either. So kids can get into it at an early age, singles and couples can enjoy both the physical exercise and the enormously sociable aspects of boating, while "experienced" sailors can carry on well into their 70s and beyond—which makes it a recreational sport that you can turn into a lifelong love affair.

To that extent, boating can be all things to all people. It's sociable, clubby (but in a good way—sailors are almost always inclined to be helpful), a great way to make like-minded friends or meet other families who share similar interests. It promotes independence and responsibility, it's terrific exercise, it puts you in touch with the natural world in a way that's more intimate than almost any other sport, and it can be combined with other pastimes like camping, fishing, watching wildlife, diving, or—let's be honest—lounging about in the sunshine, enjoying a good book, or a snooze in the afternoon.

Getting a Feel for It

In the pages that follow, we'll try and give you a sense of how boating "works," and if you're currently a newcomer to the whole thing, hopefully make it attractive enough that you'll be tempted to give it a go. As you progress, you'll read quite a lot about safety and preparedness, about checklists and practice. This isn't intended to cause alarm and shouldn't put you off, but all forms of boating can be dangerous, and it's necessary to be safe on the water at all times. For that reason we'd always recommend that anyone interested in taking up boating makes a commitment to take some lessons from a qualified instructor or experienced practitioner, so they can learn how to control their craft properly. This will make the whole experience safer for you, as well as everyone around you.

What You'll Find Here

Because there are so many different kinds of boats and so many different places to enjoy them, this book is necessarily an overview—a chance to dip your toes into the boating life a little and see if you like the feel and the sound of it. We think you will.

Along the way, the contents offer a wide range of invaluable advice about all manner of boat-related matters, from buying one to taking care of it, from transporting it to the water to launching it, from finding a place to keep it to maintaining it regularly. Most of all, the aim of this book is to give you a sense of the fun that you can have onboard a boat—any kind of boat, and wherever you choose to put it in the water.

And, although this book is an introduction, it's also designed to be a handy source of reference material that you can take with you—hence the splash-proof zip-up wallet. We hope you'll find it useful not just on your first trip, but for many years to come.

Captain Jack was right all along, you know. Boating is about freedom, and in a world where we're increasingly constrained, where things are forever being tucked up and tidied away, that's something worth remembering.

- Why Go Boating?
- Documents, Registrations, and Licenses
- When and Where
- Singles, Couples, and Families
- Is Boating for Me?
- A Day in the Life

SECTION ONE

The Basics

Why Go Boating?

Given that nearly three-quarters of the earth's surface is covered by water, in a way it would be rude not to go boating, at least once or twice. And although the oceans contain over 97 percent of the world's water, it's rare that many of us find ourselves more than an hour's drive away from some kind of lake or river, reservoir or canal, where we can enjoy a relaxing afternoon afloat.

Widely regarded as the world's most expensive hobby, and painted by some as a kind of giant aquatic money-pit into which individuals, couples, and entire families cheerfully pour their life savings, their children's inheritance, and anything else they can lay their hands on, boating nevertheless continues to grow in popularity as a hobby all over the world. Indeed, wherever there is a patch of water large enough to accommodate a boat, you'll find one there—with people in it.

So What's the Attraction?

Most enthusiasts talk about the sense of freedom that being on a boat gives them, whether they're heading out of Nassau for the Bimini Islands in the Bahamas, or ambling through Dutch canals to the famous potteries at Workum and Makkum; whether they're sea-kayaking off Vancouver Island (keeping a wary lookout for that pod of killer whales) or pottering around in a dinghy in England's picturesque Lake District. On the face of it, you couldn't really imagine environments that were more different, but you can bet that each person in

each place would enthuse in a similar way, using words and phrases like "freedom," "a sense of space," "getting away from it all," "a chance to think," and "good old-fashioned fun."

Add to that the camaraderie of boating, the famously lively social lives of those who enjoy it, and all that healthy fresh air and exercise, and you have a hobby that surpasses nearly all others. Families can create shared memories aboard that will coax a smile of recognition from even the most monosyllabic teen, while it's hard to imagine anything more romantic than smooching with your partner while the boat rocks gently beneath you. (For singles, I refer you again to the famously lively social aspects of boating.)

Moreover, boating works for everyone who can get on and off a boat. You don't have to be super-fit, and there's no age limit. You can rent a kayak for a few bucks an hour and paddle off somewhere quiet by yourself after an hour's instruction, or cruise through the British Virgin Islands on some multi-million-dollar luxury cruiser. And, of course, between these two extremes there's everything else: inflatables, punts, dinghies, skiffs, motorboats, canal boats, cabin cruisers, yachts, catamarans, ketches, schooners, powerboats, and all manner of weird and wonderful personal craft, powered and unpowered.

The final reason you should give it a go is perhaps the simplest of all: boats rock. And we're not talking in teenage vernacular here. They literally rock. Boats can give you the ride of your life, and then gently rock you to sleep, all in the same day. You don't get that in the car.

Whether you're facing gale-force winds or just pottering along sedately on a canal, being on a boat alters your perspective and makes you look at the world with fresh eyes.

What to Call Them?

So, what do you call someone who enjoys boating? It's something we wrestled with when this book was being planned. To call them sailors worried us at first, because that implied sailboats and the sea, and this book is about much more than that. People who enjoy boating do so on all manner of waters and in every type of craft. So are they boaters? Perhaps that's the best way to describe them literally, but since it's also the name of a curious kind of English straw hat popular in the late nineteenth century, it doesn't work for us either. As for the other suggestions—boatman (sexist), mariner (too formal), seafarer (too salty), shipmate (too familiar), yachtsman (sexist and "enginist")—none of them seemed to fit the bill, so for the purposes of this book, and in the full knowledge that there will be someone, somewhere who objects, we're going with the marvelously inconsistent "sailor" and "boating." This will apply to people who enjoy boats large and small, those with and without engines, on sea and freshwater, lakes and rivers, canals and reservoirs, ponds and oceans alike. We've made our peace with it, and we hope you will, too.

Documents, Registrations, and Licenses

Amazingly, there are many places in many different parts of the world where you don't need to pass any kind of competence test before going out on a boat. Even more amazingly, this applies to large, powerful, and difficult-to-handle boats just as much as it does to skiffs and dinghies. In fact, in many territories, the emphasis seems to be more on regulations that ensure the boat itself is safe, and then passing on the responsibility for personal safety to the sailor.

Let's be clear. On the one hand, the notion of personal responsibility is an exciting one, perfectly in tune with the sense of freedom that boating brings. On the other, it's in our nature to seek shortcuts, no matter how foolhardy the risks.

The most recent facts and figures from the United States Coast Guard (USCG) offer a useful snapshot of what's going on in a relatively regulated environment. Over a 12-month period there were 3,451 injuries, 697 fatalities, and about $39m worth of damage to property; of the people who drowned, 87 percent were not wearing life jackets; and alcohol intake was a factor in only one quarter of all accidents. The most reported accident types were collisions between vessels. In conclusion, the USCG offered the following comment: "Overall, carelessness/ reckless operation, operator inattention, excessive speed, and operator inexperience are the leading contributing factors in all reported accidents. About 70 percent of all boating fatalities occurred on boats where the operator had not received boating safety instruction." The message is pretty clear: even if it's not a legal

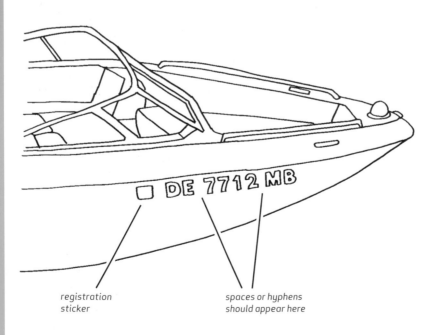

registration
sticker

spaces or hyphens
should appear here

Operating a Radio

If your boat is fitted with a hand-held or fixed radio set, you may be required to take a short, examined course to prove your competence. In the UK, for example, there's something called the Short Range Certificate (SRC), which allows you to run a Very High Frequency (VHF) radio-telephone with Digital Selective Calling (DSC). This has a one-touch emergency transmit button that sends the Maritime Mobile Service Identity number (MMSI) which is unique to your vessel. Whether you're required to hold a VHF license will depend on the territory you're boating in.

requirement, it's imperative to get some kind of training and safety instruction under your belt before you go boating.

What you actually need to learn depends very much on the kind of boating you intend to do. If you're doing something simple and basic—messing about in a little powered dinghy, or planning a canal-boat trip— then the training offered at the waterside before you set off is usually enough. In those situations you'll almost certainly be renting a boat, and common sense and a quick visual check will tell you whether the boat is properly maintained or not. If in doubt, don't go out—after all, you wouldn't drive a dangerous-looking car.

Documentation

As for documentation, in the US this varies from state to state. Alabama, for example, requires that every person who drives a motorized boat has boater safety certification, but doesn't ask the same of people who

use sailboats, rowboats, or canoes. California, on the other hand, has no safety course or training requirements, while Florida lets over-21s pilot vessels of 10 horsepower or above without a boater education course.

In the UK, there's no formal requirement for any kind of license at all, though the Royal Yachting Association (RYA) recommends you ask yourself the following questions: "Will I get the boat back safely?" and "Will the boat get me back safely?" If you're unable to answer "yes" to both questions, you should take one of the RYA's many training courses, which cater for all age groups and ranges of experience, from absolute beginners right up to those who'd like to train as instructors.

Mainland Europe is home to some of the most extensive and beautiful river and canal systems in the world, and many countries require an International Certificate of Competence (ICC). You may well need separate

Alcohol should be viewed with suspicion on a boat, and in some territories it is simply banned. Know the limits and stick to them.

qualifications to sail on their inland waterways (pleasure-boat licenses are a requirement in France, for example); most territories require that your boat is licensed and registered.

The upshot of all this is that you need to be aware that there will be regulations governing the use of boats, no matter where in the world you are, and that it's your responsibility to be familiar with them.

SECTION ONE

When and Where

If your notion of boating is a yacht tied up to an exclusive marina in the south of France, or bobbing at anchor against an azure Caribbean sky, then you've got many alternative versions of the waterborne experience waiting for you. The fact is, if you have the necessary paperwork, and have passed the relevant courses, you can sail anywhere there's enough water to put a boat.

Ponds

Familiar with the phrase "big fish in a small pond?" The same applies when it comes to boats, so you need to be realistic and match the size of your craft to the size of the water you wish to introduce it to. Smaller waters may have more rules than larger ones, because their ecosystems are more easily damaged—many ponds, for example, ban internal combustion engines—and, as always, it's up to you to find out what the rules are, and then comply with them. You need to be especially considerate toward others as well, if you're intending to have your fun in such a confined space.

Lakes and Reservoirs

Again, you'll need to discover and follow any local rules, and be on the lookout for areas designated for swimmers and other water users, so you can steer clear of them. Be especially careful of anglers using inflatable float tubes, because they can turn up in out-of-the-way places, and they sit low in the water, which makes them hard to see. Some lakes impose speed limits on boat owners—which makes them unsuitable for waterskiing—while others won't have any facilities for launching boats, apart from craft like kayaks and canoes.

Canals

For beginners, canals have many advantages over rivers, mainly because they're straight, slow-running, and wonderfully predictable. In fact, in some places you can rent a canal boat or a cruiser without any previous experience and

14

be taught how to operate it there and then. With an average top speed of 3 mph, there's usually time to make any adjustments necessary to avoid other boats—which, of course, are often only traveling as fast as you are. Moorings are usually free (unless they're clearly private property), and locks are relatively easy to negotiate once you've gone through a couple. Mainland Europe can be a little different, because there are many more signs, many more locks, and heavy traffic—you'll be expected to pass the equivalent of a driving test.

Rivers

Somewhat less predictable than canals, rivers offer more of a challenge to the beginner, whether under sail, in a small cruiser, experiencing the

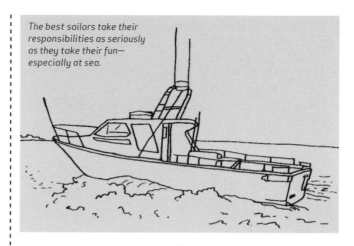

The best sailors take their responsibilities as seriously as they take their fun—especially at sea.

thrill of white-water rafting as a group, or kayaking by yourself or with friends. The characteristics of a river can change quickly and are influenced by a wide range of factors, including width, depth, and the amount of water flowing through; there are also more likely to be unforeseen hazards due to erosion, such as collapsed banks and fallen trees. You may also have to pay some kind of registration fee if you own a boat and want to take it on the river.

Estuaries

These can offer the perfect halfway house between the relative comfort of a river and the wildness of the open sea. An estuary is body of water formed by the mixing of fresh and sea water, and is therefore tidal, which beginners need to watch out for. But estuaries give you a marvelous taste of the sea, while still protecting you from the full force of

the tides and the wind, which makes them good fun for powered vessels and excellent places to learn the basics of sailing. One caveat: estuary mud is one of the stickiest substances on earth, and will stick to you and your boat like glue.

The Sea

This is the real thing, and needs to be treated with respect, partly because there are so many people using it—often driving high-powered vessels of one kind or another. Seriously, never venture out to sea unless you are confident that you can control your boat safely, know where you are going, and know how to return safely. Taking a boat out to sea with no qualifications or experience, or without someone on board who knows what they're doing, is utterly irresponsible.

Singles, Couples, and Families

There's no such thing as the typical sailor or the typical crew. There are as many types of sailors as there are boats to sail in, and no matter what your circumstances, you'll find there's enormous enjoyment to be had on your own, with a partner, or in a group.

Sailing Solo

Sailing alone on most kinds of inland water requires only that you exercise reasonable care. Should you be traveling into the middle of nowhere, it's important that you have enough experience, and take some simple precautions:

• Tell friends where you're going, and arrange to contact them on your return.
• If sailing in a national park or wilderness area, make sure you fill in any relevant paperwork that may be required for the trip.

• Make sure you have well-maintained equipment, including a first-aid kit that you know how to use.

The challenges involved increase dramatically when you put to sea. Only experienced sailors should head out into the open sea on their own. Solo sailing also introduces practical limits to the kind of vessel you can transport, launch, and control.

Wherever you are, you're going to get tired because you'll be running the boat on your own. Obviously, the degree of tiredness you're likely to experience will vary depending on what you're doing. Kayaking or ocean sailing is really going to take it out of you, while canal-boat "captains" rarely exhibit signs of fatigue. Remember that you'll also be spending time on your own getting to and from the water, and, depending on the journey, that can result in long, solitary days; still, solo sailors enjoy the extra sense of freedom that being alone on the water brings, and often find it addictively satisfying.

Couples Afloat

Sailing is perfect for couples. It gives you a shared sense of purpose and encourages you to spend time actually doing something together, instead of slumping in front of the TV. Sailing couples are fully engaged with the world around them and are more likely to enjoy an active and healthy lifestyle than their shorebound friends. Two is also a perfect number for manning a small boat on inland waters or at sea, where there are plenty of jobs to be shared and where speed of thought and concentration are as valuable as strength and stamina.

Sailing together expands the range of vessels and environments that you can enjoy. Transporting the boat becomes easier: there's nearly always some lugging to be done, and two pairs of hands are better than one. It's best to divide the jobs in some way so that each person has set responsibilities. Although it may take time for you both to settle into a routine on board, it's immensely satisfying to work as a team, and the number of couples who take up sailing—even to the extent of selling their house and living on a boat—increases every year.

If one partner is uncertain about the idea, then it's best to start with a short, easy trip; this is nearly always more successful than going overboard (not literally, of course) on the luxury side of things, particularly if that kind of extravagance is typically beyond your budget. A few short trips in the summer to a local lake or canal—or even a novice-friendly bay—will often do the trick.

Family Fun

Given how hard it is to get the family together to do anything these days, pouring them into a boat for an hour, an afternoon, or a week's boating trip, is the perfect solution—if only because once on board they can't get away from each other. Seriously, kids love boats. If you give them jobs—and you should—they learn responsibility. They learn how to steer or row, which ropes to pull on (and which ones to avoid), and they learn how to cooperate and rub along with their brothers and sisters in a way that's both confident and accommodating. Kids will put up with a lot when they're on a boat. They won't mind sharing or helping out, and there's less time and space for tantrums and sulks, and more time for fun and games.

It's also great for parents, because you get to teach your kids stuff—real stuff that you can watch them put to good use straight away. There's nothing quite like teaching a kid to steer a little powered dinghy and then settling back as they take it, and you, around the lake for a spin.

Is Boating for Me?

Unless that lottery win is burning a hole in your pocket, it's unlikely that you'll be going out to buy any kind of boat before you've had a few trial runs. So what's the best way to find out whether the life afloat is for you or not? Here are a few suggestions to get you started.

Clubs

Although sailing clubs are undoubtedly one of the best places to start, you may have to seek out one that actively welcomes beginners; many of them seem overly concerned with keeping their current members happy, rather than trying to attract new ones. A good club will offer recognized courses for beginners, as well as a lively social scene with plenty of opportunities for you to meet and mix with others who are just starting out. Look for clubs that run introductory or "get-acquainted" days.

Outdoor Activity Centers

There are a great many opportunities to rent different kinds of small boats by the hour, and get some training at the same time. Alternatively, plan ahead and book a proper session to learn about white-water kayaking or dinghy sailing. If you live near the water, you may find that prices are cheaper off-season.

Sailing Vacations

There is a wide variety of vacations to suit every style of boating and every budget, and they're a great way to find out whether or not you want to take this up seriously. Back-to-nature vacations often have interesting water-based activities available, and there are vast networks of inland waterways waiting to be explored by canal boat or motor cruiser, both of which require minimal training. Further afield, lots of travel companies run residential courses, sometimes in spectacular locations, where you can learn to sail as well as touching up your tan. Of course, unless you're very

Seasickness

The French call it *mal de mer*, which makes it sound rather tame, but sufferers know just how hideous it can be.

First, there's no need to be embarrassed. It's said that almost half of all astronauts suffer from the airborne equivalent—space sickness—and have to take medication for it. Seasickness has very little to do with your stomach—rather, it's to do with the way that your brain tries to deal with different stimuli. What happens is that the signals sent by the body, the eyes, and most importantly, the inner ear, tend to conflict with each other, causing confusion. Your inner ear tells you that you're moving, while your eyes look at the objects all around and tell you that these are stable—and that therefore you're not moving. When the two stimuli collide, the result is nausea, and your body reacts by trying to empty the contents of your stomach.

Seasickness usually passes in a day or so when people get their "sea legs." If not, over-the-counter medicines will usually do the trick. Until you find your sea legs, avoid the following:

- Focusing on one thing, like a book or magazine—this reinforces the confusion between what the eye sees (a static object) and the constant movement the inner ear feels.

- Using binoculars— curiously, this produces exactly the same effect, because your eyes are framed by something fixed while everything else is moving like crazy.
- Going below deck for long periods.
- Strong smells—no one's quite sure why, unless it's just the result of yet another sense thrown into the already confused sensory mix.

Many sailors have found that eating ginger biscuits can help seasickness. The strong taste and tang of the ginger is a powerful, natural remedy. Alternatively, some people swear by acupressure wrist bands (*left*), which you just slip over each wrist and then forget about. Focusing on the horizon helps, as does lying down on your back and closing your eyes.

fortunate, the sailing back home may not be as exotic. This is worth remembering, as people can be seduced by the environment rather than boating, and become disillusioned when trying it back home.

Books and DVDs

Although both can help you to familiarize yourself with the different parts of a boat, or with the principles of how sails interact with the wind, how to steer, and so on, there's simply

no substitute for practical, hands-on lessons. You can use books and multimedia to support your learning by all means, but don't rely solely on them.

SECTION ONE

A Day in the Life

Talk to any sailor and they'll tell you that there's no such thing as a typical day. They'll also explain that this is part of the beauty of boating—that the unexpected is always just around the corner, and that a lot of the fun comes from trying to anticipate what's going to happen next. That said, every trip requires a little planning, and there are usually a few regular jobs that need doing, no matter what kind of boat you're setting out on.

The Night Before

Just as your boat needs fuel (whether it's gasoline for the engine or wind for the sails), so do the people on board. Vittles—or victuals, as they should properly be called—are the provisions for your trip, and can be prepared the night before. A picnic in a cooler is fine for a day trip, maybe with a flask or two of hot drinks to keep everyone's spirits up if the weather turns bad. Alcohol is rarely forbidden on a boat, but should be treated with the same caution as you'd use if you were driving a car. If you're planning to be away for more than a day, you'll need to plan some menus and work out how much food to carry; turn to Section Five for everything you need to know about provisioning and cooking on a boat. You should also plan where you're going, and estimate the time required.

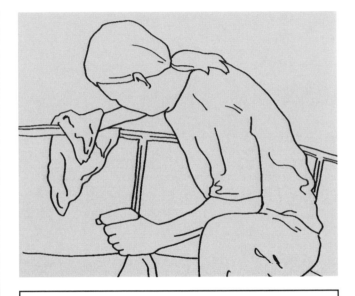

First Thing

Any exposed areas of the boat that are wet with dew should be dried with a chamois-leather cloth; take special care with the windows and any brightwork. Use a rain-repellent cleaner on your windows, and wipe these down with a chamois as well. We'll cover the full pre-cast-off checklist on page 50, but, depending on your vessel, you may need to check fuel and oil levels before you go, and make sure you carry enough to top the tanks up as required. You'll also need lots of drinking water; see page 79 for details.

Before You Leave

Do a weather check, look at tide tables if you need to, select any necessary charts, and keep them close at hand. Finally, run your boat safety checks, damage check, and radio check. All of these will be covered in detail on pages 42–44. Stow away any items that aren't secured, and check for personal flotation devices, flares, and a first-aid kit. Make sure the deck's clear.

Underway

You should keep a log, even on an afternoon pleasure cruise, because it's a lot of fun. More seriously, you should log your position every 20 minutes or so; this is not just a useful journal of record, but can be crucial in the event of an accident and insurance claim. You should also set regular watches, even when you're out on the local lake for fun; kids, especially, enjoy the responsibility of being in charge of something, and it'll stand them in good stead later on, should they become more serious about boating. While you're underway you may find yourself carrying out all sorts of routine maintenance, such as plugging a leak, mending a puncture in an inflatable, changing the various bulbs on board, switching on navigation lights, recharging boat batteries, practicing maneuvers like tacking and jibbing, checking the rigging, and so on.

At the End of the Day

If you've started with the idea that you're either going to be steering or sailing the boat, or just kicking back while others have a go, then life on board may come as something of a shock. Despite spending most of the time in the water, boats do not clean themselves; the "crew" (even if there's only one of you) takes care of that. Hosing down the deck, general cleaning, and taking care of the head (toilet) are all usually done at the end of the day. If you're fortunate enough to have teak surfaces, these need special care; if they're oiled, then use a teak cleaner and dry them after washing the boat. Wash the boat down after each use to remove salt and dirt, and run your fingers over the surfaces to see if you need to add a mild detergent. You should also check ropes regularly for signs of wear, wash them with a mild detergent to remove salt, and coil and hang them properly after use, rather than just spooling them on the deck, where they'll get in everyone's way.

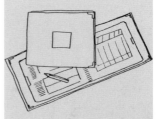

A logbook is a vital piece of equipment. No matter what kind of boating you do, know how to use it, and keep it up to date.

SECTION TWO

The Boat

Different Kinds of Boats

There are as many different kinds of vessel as there are waters on which to enjoy them. Though we won't go into the very expensive or highly specialized types on these pages, we will look at the major boat types and some of their variations, in an attempt to demonstrate what's offered to the first-time sailor. Many of these boats will be available second-hand, and thrifty would-be owners would do well to consider buying that way, at least for a first purchase.

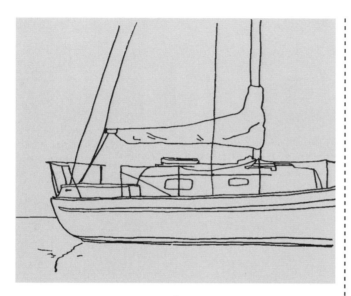

This means that out of all the boats considered in this book, the sailboat is the one that absolutely needs lessons. Now, this doesn't necessarily mean spending a fortune getting qualifications, but safety on the water should be everyone's primary concern. A sailboat—even a little dinghy—is too complicated to get into on your own for the first time and just think you can sail off into the sunset, and then expect to come back. Yes, many sailboats do have engines, but these are for emergencies, or for maneuvering in and out of tight spaces.

Sailboat

Types include: dinghy, catamaran, trimaran, catboat, cutter, sloop, ketch.

Sailboats are the most demanding of all vessels to master. That's not to say that piloting a sailboat is rocket science (though actually it is mostly science), but that sailors spend a lot of time learning how to make a boat go in one direction when the wind wants it to go in the other. This means that, along with canoeing and kayaking, running a sailboat is one of the most physically demanding types of boating you can do.

Although there are dozens of different types of sailboat in many different sizes, they all share the same basic characteristics: a hull, a mast, sails, and devices under the water, attached to the hull, for steering and to stop them toppling over. The way these basic components are arranged is what differentiates one kind of sailboat from another. Having mastered one type of sailboat you'll be prepared to steer another—but only to the extent that having passed your driving test in a compact car, will allow you to drive something like a truck.

FOR: There's a big close-to-nature thing that goes on with sailboats—harnessing the power of the wind to go where you want. It's clean power, exhilarating, and can have a relatively low cost of entry for beginners.

AGAINST: Can be physically demanding, difficult at first, and it requires patience and concentration.

craft when compared with a sailing boat—even one of a similar size. Exactly how the accommodation is arranged will depend on the size and age of the boat, but generally you'll be more comfortable. There'll be more room on deck as well, with plenty of different seating and lounging areas. There is, of course, no typical layout, but you can expect two single beds in the bow that can be combined to make a double, a small galley, head (toilet) and shower, one or more couches that convert into single beds, a combined living/dining area, and plenty of closet space. Larger boats may add a second head and another pair of single-into-double beds.

Motorboat

Types include: powerboat, ski-boat (designed for use with waterskis and wakeboards), bow rider, cabin cruiser, motor cruiser, luxury motor yacht.

Often referred to cruelly by sailboat owners as the "motor homes of the sea," motorboats are the natural habitat of those who embrace the life afloat for the amount of enjoyment it provides. Motorboat owners are thus often less interested in harnessing the power of the wind to glide silently beneath the stars, and more interested in sunbathing, fishing, snorkeling, and generally having a good time.

Because of the way they're designed, you can expect more room and more home comforts from a pleasure

Single or Twin Engines?

A twin-engine motorboat has a number of advantages over one equipped with a single engine. Number one, if the first engine fails, you've got something to fall back on. It's also easier to maneuver with two engines, particularly if you're fighting both wind and current, and you're in a tight space. Finally, you can go further and faster, so you can stay out longer. The drawback is obvious: you use twice as much fuel and emit twice as much gunk into the water and the atmosphere. The choice is yours!

FOR: Comfort, space, range; more suitable if you sail with a specific purpose in mind; for example, fishing, or diving in a particular spot.

AGAINST: You're more cocooned and more reliant on technology; the boat is more expensive to run, noisy, and—compared with a sailboat—more polluting.

Different Kinds of Boats continued

Canal Boat

Also called: narrowboat, houseboat.

There are several factors that distinguish a canal boat from any other object of a would-be sailor's affections. First, it's bigger than most of the boats that most of us can afford. Second, it's more sedate (apart from some sections of Europe's busiest inland waterways). And third, many owners choose to live on their boats or to boat-share with others. Owning a canal boat is at least as big a lifestyle commitment as owning a good-sized sailboat and using it regularly.

Of course, canal boats have comfort on their side, and this makes them attractive to the kind of people who shudder at the conditions "endured" on other kinds of boat. Owners can expect to enjoy several rooms, carpets, hot water, appliances—even central heating!

Outside, the main difference between canal boats is the way the stern is arranged. The traditional narrowboat carries the roof almost to the tiller and leaves room for one—at most two—people to stand and steer the boat, while the newer "cruiser" style has a much larger outside space in front of the tiller. A semitraditional design offers the benefits of a large rear deck, but encloses them with walls (rather than rails) so that from the outside it looks like a traditional boat.

FOR: Comfort, relaxation, a life lived on the water, thousands upon thousands of miles of canals to explore.

AGAINST: May be too sedate for some; unless you're continuously cruising, you'll need a permanent mooring; it's a lot of boat to look after.

Personal Watercraft

Personal watercraft (or PWCs) such as Jet Skis® use a motor to suck water in and then propel it out the back with enormous force. They are very popular with beginners—and thieves, so make sure yours is secure, electronically tagged, and so on. Note that some inland waters have strict regulations about acceptable emission levels, so check before you go

their back to the direction of travel, and the oars pivot on an oarlock (rowlock).

FOR: Relatively low cost of ownership, fantastic exercise, can go pretty much anywhere.

AGAINST: Unstable until you get the hang of it, demands that you are reasonably fit.

Rowboat

Types include: canoe, kayak.

Although there are all sorts of specialized variations, the two most popular types of rowboat are the canoe, which has a simple, open design with no deck, and the kayak, which has a covered deck with a little hole in it for the rower's body, protected by a spray cover or spray deck to stop the water getting in. As a rule, canoes are used in gentler water, while kayaks are favored in rougher conditions (such as whitewater) or at sea. However, there are now so many kayak variations that can carry more than one person, or are molded so that you sit on top, or have a small sail or electric motor, that, assuming your watercraft is up to scratch, they can be used almost anywhere. There are also plenty of canoes that break the traditional mold and feature decks, small sails, and engines. However, the majority are still enjoyed in the old-fashioned way and are popular for touring backwoods and wilderness areas, where their larger capacity makes them more suitable for campers, hunters, and anglers who are hauling lots of gear.

Both canoes and kayaks use oars or paddles for propulsion, but these are designed differently and employ different techniques. Kayakers have a single, long, double-ended oar that is gripped in the center, while canoeists use a smaller, single-ended oar.

The traditional flat-bottomed rowboat is now mostly seen on lakes and ponds, or used to move between the shore and a larger boat. The main difference here is that the person doing the rowing has

Inflatables

Also known as rubber dinghies, these are boats constructed out of flexible inflatable tubes which can be packed down for easy transportation and then inflated again at the waterside. They can be used with small outboard engines or oars, and are increasingly popular among whitewater rafters. Anglers and divers like them, and they're still widely used for getting people on and off larger boats. Rigid inflatable boats (RIBs) are often used for sea rescue by the emergency services. The float tube is a very small inflatable for personal use, favored by some anglers.

Buying a Boat

So you've considered your options, had some lessons, maybe taken a skippered weekend break or a cruising trip, and you're well and truly besotted. Your shorebound days are behind you, and in front lies the kind of freedom that only a boat can deliver. The next step, then, is to buy your own. But how do you know a good one from a bad one? Before you buy, have a look at our checklist of things to watch out for.

What's It For?

The most important consideration when buying a boat is to know what kind you want and where you're going to use it. By "kind," we don't mean make and model number, but whether it's an ocean-going vessel for your year's sabbatical from work, a kayak for a whitewater trip, a dinghy for a day out at the local lake, or a canal boat to live on. Once you've made your mind up, make sure that the person you're trying to buy the boat from also understands what you're going to use it for.

Where to Go?

It may sound obvious, but boat shows are great places to buy a boat. There will be many different kinds to choose from, and there are usually so many special offers that it's actually possible to secure a good deal for yourself, or at least get plenty of added extras included in the end price. Alternatively, look at boat dealers on the Internet or those with a local presence, and check local marinas, sailing clubs, boating magazines, and flyers for boats for sale.

Things to Remember

- As you're buying the boat, think about how easy it's going to be to sell it again; like unusual houses, unusual boats may be full of character, but they'll always appeal to fewer people.

- Resist any efforts to make you put money down on the spot to get a good deal; never let yourself be rushed into anything.
- If you need to finance the purchase, a specialist lender will typically give you a better deal—they'll certainly be better acquainted with what's involved.
- Do the math. The initial outlay on the boat is only part of the equation—you'll also have to equip it, maintain it, repair it, and run it—not to mention insure it.
- Don't wear your Sunday best; go prepared to inspect any out-of-the-way places on the boat.
- Try out everything to make sure it works. Don't be shy—be sure to check the engine, bilge, controls (especially the steering), propeller and propeller shaft, batteries, fuel tanks, electrical components, and the condition of the hull, rigging, and sails.
- Just as you wouldn't buy a car without trying it out, you should expect to be able to take your new boat for a test.
- In most cases, you'll need a written assessment of the boat's condition from a qualified marine surveyor before you can get insurance. If you've never been in charge of a boat before, tie in the test drive with the inspection; that way you can get the inspector to take you out.
- When you're insuring your boat, get a separate policy

Can I Afford a Boat?

There's a great story about boats and boating that does the rounds from time to time and is worth repeating here. The owner of a boat is treating a non-boating friend to a trip around the lake, the bay, or wherever the story happens to be set. The friend remarks: "You're very lucky. I'd really love to have a boat like this." The captain of the boat smiles, takes out his wallet, and quite deliberately begins to remove bills at random and drop them over the side. His friend looks on in horror. "What are you doing?" he says, grabbing him by the arm. "If you can't afford to do this," replies the captain, "then a boat is the last thing you need."

That may sound more negative than it's supposed to. The real issue is this: given the years of pleasure that you, your partner, friends, and family can look forward to, can you afford *not* to own a boat?

rather than, for example, adding it to your homeowner's policy. This will give you better coverage. For insurance purposes, "boats" are usually considered to be 26 ft long or less, while "yachts" are anything longer.
- If this is your first boat, think about where you're going to keep it. Boats that can be stored and transported on a trailer behind a car are much more convenient—and thus more likely to be used—than those that can't.

Understanding Your Boat

Although each boat works in a different way, they all share similar characteristics. For example, the bow and stern of a boat are in the same place whether you're on a 37 ft yacht or a 6 ft motor dinghy. But, as with any specialized subject, there's a bit of useful jargon to learn, so you may as well start learning it now.

Let's start by looking at some the basic component parts of pretty much every boat.

The **hull** comprises everything from the deck down. The **bow** is the front end of the vessel, while the **stern** is the back end (sometimes called the **aft** end); the **beam** is the widest point of the boat, while the **draft** is the minimum depth of water the boat needs to float properly, usually measured as the distance between the lowest part of the hull and the waterline. The **freeboard** is the distance between the deck and the surface of the water, while the **gunwhale**—pronounced "gunnel"—is the top edge of the boat's hull.

When the Wind Blows

Though it's less of an issue with a powered vessel, wind direction is crucial to sailing boats, and there are some important bits of jargon to know about. The **lee** is the direction the wind is blowing from, and the **leeward** side is the side of the boat that is sheltered from the wind; the **windward** side, on the other hand, is the side of the boat that the wind is blowing into.

Displacement hulls are round-bottomed and work by literally displacing the water around them. In fact, if you were able to weigh the water displaced by a boat with a hull like this, you'd discover that it weighed exactly the same as the boat. They are commonly used on slower craft that need less propulsion.

Planing hulls have bottoms that are flat or slightly V-shaped, and are designed to rise up through the water as their speed increases, until they skim across the top. Planing hulls travel faster than displacement hulls and are usually found on powered vessels.

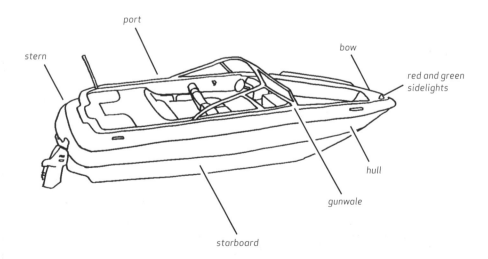

port

stern

bow

red and green sidelights

hull

gunwale

starboard

Which Way is Which?

When a boat gets underway, you'll find that sailors have their own lingo for the different directions. Here's how to work them out:

Stand in the center of the boat, facing forward. From this position, the left side of the boat is the **port** side, and the right side of the boat is the **starboard** side. **Ahead** is directly in front of the vessel, and **astern** refers to whatever is behind the vessel. **Dead ahead** and **dead astern** refer to those areas directly in front or behind. **Abeam** refers to a direction at right angles to dead ahead or dead astern at the widest point of the boat.

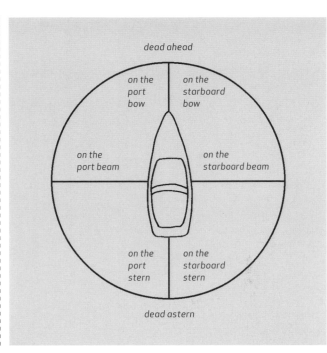

Sailboats

This picture shows several components that you'll mainly find in sailboats:

- **Mast**: the upright pole to which the sails are attached.
- **Mainsail**: the large sail behind the mast, usually the aftmost one, attached by its front edge.
- **Headsail**: any sail that is set up in front of the mainsail; the most common type of headsail is a jib.
- **Boom**: the horizontal pole that sits at right angles to the mast and supports the bottom of the mainsail.
- **Tiller**: the lever at the stern of the boat that controls the rudder (many modern sailboats have a wheel that does the same thing).
- **Rudder**: a steering fin that extends vertically into the water at the back of the boat and is controlled by the tiller.
- **Keel:** a heavily ballasted fin that runs along the middle of the bottom of the hull and keeps the boat stable; twin keels (sometimes called bilge keels) are popular in tidal areas because they let the boat stand upright when the tide's out without any additional support.

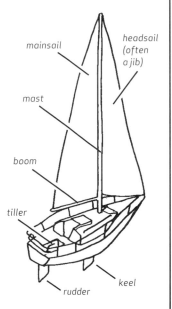

The Boating Year

In the previous chapter we looked at a typical day in the life of a boat, and now we're going to try and get some idea of the kinds of things that go on in a typical boating year. Of course, one of the attractions of life afloat is that it's always changing, and when you throw in the fact that there are many hundreds of different kinds of boats, and millions of different locations, and thousands of different environments, you'll never get a typical anything. But if you could…

Spring

This is when the boating season starts. At this time, you can expect to see people giving their vessels a good spring-clean and carrying out general maintenance.

Jobs: Cleaning, oiling, polishing, painting, and varnishing the deck, toe rails, spray hoods, deck, stanchions, and shrouds; servicing inboard and outboard engines; checking the bilge pump, fire extinguishers, life jackets, life raft, flares, torches, and cooking appliances. You'll also change oil filters and check for damaged hoses and the like. If you're planning a long trip, then there's plenty to do, including making a travel plan, collecting the relevant documentation, checking the requirements of sailing abroad, taking that final course, and taking one-day trips in challenging weather in order to get yourself mentally and physically prepared.

Fun Stuff: Now's the time to join a club and go sailing, boating, canoeing, windsurfing, kite-surfing, and rowing, or get in touch with a local owners' association and get to know people with boats like yours. Clubs will offer you the opportunity to race or go to regattas, or maybe crew on someone else's boat.

Summer and Fall

As the weather improves, so do the opportunities for fun. However, maintaining a good and safe boat is an ongoing job, so keep up the good work.

Jobs: As before.

Fun Stuff: Check out your local club and you'll see that the competitions, races, rallies, regattas, and club days out just keep on coming. Take the boat out for the day and drop anchor while you swim and fish. Practice your person-overboard drill and then wind down with an on-deck barbecue. Fancy taking a course? Both the Mediterranean and the Caribbean are favorite destinations at this time of year, particularly for sailors who want to improve their skills. Alternatively, go sports fishing, take a canal trip in Holland, go rowing on the Thames in England, or just treat yourself to some fun on a Jet Ski®.

Winter

OK, fun's over—actually, not quite. But in the winter months, you'll find some of the time taken up with the

larger, more long-term maintenance work that keeps a boat in good condition.

Jobs: Most of these need to be done when the boat is out of the water and on a trailer, or in a shed or boatyard. Boats that have been used in salt water will need anti-fouling treatment to remove any marine organisms—slime, barnacles, mussels, seaweed spores, and assorted other gunk—that have become attached, like unwanted hitchhikers, to the hull of the boat. Fouling not only makes your boat look bad but actually slows it down, makes it harder to maneuver and less fuel-efficient. After that, you can repaint the hull, sand and revarnish/repaint wooden areas, then think

about any new equipment you might want to install, like a radio, a new mast, or new window hatches. Fill the gas tank to avoid condensation and oxidization, and then change the oil. If your engine needs coolant, drain what's there and replace it with one of the newer glycol-based antifreezes, which are more environmentally friendly; then take out the battery and take it home. Remember that the winter months are long, and it's better to do the protective work at the beginning of the season rather than waiting until spring arrives.

Fun Stuff: Plan a last trip around an exciting natural event—a lunar eclipse, meteor showers, the northern lights—or go whale or dolphin watching. Go fishing for those hardy species like cod or bass in the sea, or pike and muskies in lakes, rivers, and ponds. Get involved in a conservation project, or just help yourself to all that empty water, now that the fair-weather sailors have packed up for the year!

Mooring

It's an inconvenient fact of life that you can't be on the water enjoying yourself every day of the week. And that means you have to have somewhere to keep your boat. And since you'll want access to it whenever the mood takes you—or the weather takes a turn for the better—then a mooring is definitely the way to go. But how do you organize one?

of opportunities can come up—especially the chance to help out on a boat much larger than your own. It's a great way to gain experience.

• **A Marina**
Again you'll pay an annual fee, but look for the following to be included: the dockage itself, spring launch and fall haul-out, a fall bottom wash (for the boat), winter cradle storage, pump-outs for the season, and the use of the marina's facilities—laundry, showers, maybe a pool, a gym, or tennis courts.

• **River and Canal Moorings**
Although you can often tie up where you like for an hour or two—or even overnight—permanent moorings on running water are harder to come by. Your best bet is to try a local club, or contact the local authorities for advice. You'll also find enormous local variations—for example, many people who have boats in the Mediterranean take them up into France for the winter, where they pay only a flat rate to cruise the canal system. There are also "bottom of the garden" moorings for those whose property backs onto water.

On page 35 we'll be singing the praises of trailer boating, but it does have one distinct disadvantage—aside from maybe having to take the roof off your garage—and that's this: when you keep your boat actually on the water you've always got an excuse to go and visit it—or the club house at the marina, or the bait shop on the lake, or the park ranger's office. You'd be amazed at the number of

boats that get parked up in a garage or put into storage and then forgotten about.

If you want to moor your boat, then your choices are:

• **A Sailing or Boating Club**
After paying an annual mooring fee, club members will usually get a better deal on boat storage. Clubs have decent facilities, and by regularly mixing with other members all sorts

Trailers and Boats

One of the key factors in choosing a boat is how you store it and get it to and from the water. If you can fit the boat onto a trailer and then tow it with the same automobile you use every day, you'll be at an enormous advantage when it comes to choosing when and where to enjoy your hobby.

A boat that fits on a trailer opens up so many more possibilities for the sailor than one that needs to live in a marina or go into professional winter storage. For a start, it gives you fantastic flexibility in terms of when and where you can go sailing—you wake up on the weekend, the weather's taken an unexpected turn for the better, you pack a few bits and pieces, and you're on the road, heading for your favorite lake, or with the map out, looking for new waters to explore. It makes the whole experience less complicated and more immediate.

Clearly, not every car can tow every boat, so you'll need to do a little homework first. Your vehicle owner's manual should have its towing capacity somewhere in there, and you can always call your dealer if in doubt. Then check the boat manual to get the weight of the boat, and see if they match up within an acceptable level of tolerance. Remember that the boat manual may only list what's called the "dry" weight of the boat—i.e. minus fuel and gear—so add some extra weight onto that when you're making your calculations. Obviously it depends on lots of factors, but as a rule a modern pickup or SUV (Sports Utility Vehicle) can tow a trailer and a boat of around 25 ft (7.5m) comfortably. As always, it's up to you to make sure that your trailer complies with local safety regulations— you'll certainly need brake, tail, and clearance lights.

Before You Go

• **Check** tire pressure on car and trailer; also check brakes.

• **Check** wiring is properly connected and allows room for making turns.

• **Check** all car and trailer lights—have someone stand behind and help.

• **Check** visibility in mirrors.

• **Check** the boat is secured on the trailer, and then have someone double-check it for you, especially if you've tied it on using your own knots.

• **Check** you've got wheel chocks with you for when you get to the water.

• **Check** the route for width or height restrictions.

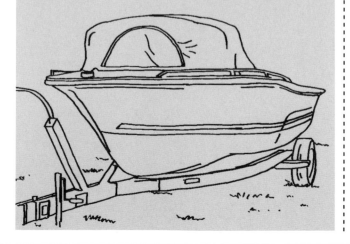

Storing Your Boat

Even the most fanatical sailor can't be on the water all the time—at some point you have to stop, even if it's only so that you can earn more money in order to go out on the water again. So, what's the best way of keeping your boat in good condition if it needs to be stored out of the water for any length of time? As ever, it depends, but here are a few suggestions to try for size:

- You can just turn it upside down—seriously. It depends on the kind of boat, but if it's a dinghy or other type of small wooden boat, it works perfectly well. Just prop it up on some cinder blocks, or something so that the air can circulate, and the hull becomes the roof—simple.

- You can trailer it and cover it. If your boat fits on a trailer, then you've got all sorts of advantages. Assuming it doesn't tower over the house next door, blocking their sunlight, there's nothing to stop you from keeping your boat in your driveway, safely cosseted under its tarpaulin. This is cheap, and also allows you, and your friendly neighbors, to keep an eye on the boat. If you've got good garage space, that's even better, as it'll keep the boat safely out of sight from potential thieves.

- It is possible to get your boat stored professionally in a sort of boat warehouse. This will be a large, secured building with racks on the walls that can take boats three or four high, which are raised into place by a forklift truck. This has the advantage of being secure, but it can be less easy to take the boat out on a whim —should spring come early, for example—and it's harder to do any maintenance on the boat. Fancy boats may need a little more tender loving care, in which case it's possible to purchase space in a heated storage facility, though this is much more expensive.

- Large boats may be kept in what's called a "wet dock," which is an area of a marina where the level is artificially maintained by a lock or series of locks. It's sometimes called a "boat well." The main issue here is water temperature—it's not advisable to store a boat in water that's likely to freeze.

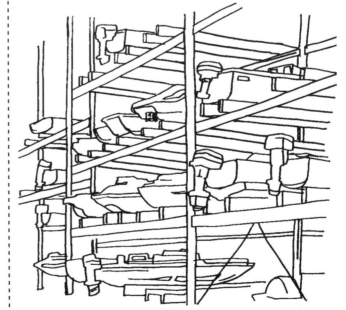

Insuring Your Boat

Just like a house or a car, your boat needs insurance to protect it from ... well, life, really. Boats are delicate things, especially when they're out of the water, or when they're being taken in and out of the water, and you need to be sure that your investment is protected; it's for your own benefit and that of other water users.

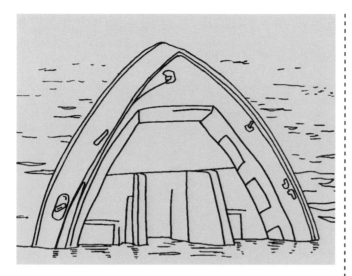

Damage and Liability

There are essentially two strands to boat insurance. The first—as you can probably guess—concerns accidental damage or loss that affects the entire boat or its components. This covers not just the big stuff like the hull, the deck, and the keel, but the sails, the engine, the anchor, rudder, cleats, or anything that's necessary in order to run the boat. The second is all to do with liability, and is there to protect you and other water users from damage, injury, or loss of life that may be caused directly or indirectly by you and/or your boat. Remember that this may need to include things like towing away the wreck of your boat, or containing and cleaning up any spilled fuel or other pollutants.

What's It Worth?

Policies with less expensive premiums use a measure known as "actual cash value" when estimating how much should be paid out in the event of damage or an accident. If the boat is of a certain age, this may well turn out not to be enough to pay for a replacement component. If the boat is damaged beyond repair, then you'll get the current market value for it, taking into account any wear and tear or depreciation. Policies that use an "agreed value" as the measure will be more expensive, but will usually allow you to replace a damaged old component with an equivalent new one. Not all parts of a boat are created equal, either, so there may well be special cases made for those items that depreciate more quickly than others (for example, a sail will probably wear out in less time than a steering wheel).

Extras

You may also wish to add "extras" to a policy, such as those personal belongings you take with you on the boat when you go fishing or diving, but that are not normally kept on the boat. Similarly, it's worth looking at some kind of coverage for towing, should you experience mechanical trouble that's inconvenient rather than life-threatening—for example, when the engine breaks down and you just need help to get home.

Note that this is only general advice, and you should consult your insurer to purchase the cover that best suits you and your boat.

- Basic Safety Rules
- Vessel Safety Check
- Provisioning the Galley
- Clothing

- Activities Checklist
- Pre-Cast-Off Checklist
- First-Aid Kit

SECTION THREE

Equipping Your Boat

Basic Safety Rules

Before we get into specific checklists about particular elements of safety when you're on the water, there are some more basic rules to consider. Although you may think that the open sea is perhaps a more dangerous place than the canal or the village pond, accidents can happen in the most familiar of places, and time spent thinking about staying safe is never wasted.

Most of this stuff is common sense—or at least you'd think it was. However, when you spend time on the water you'll discover that there are all sorts of people who behave as if they're the only ones afloat and pay little attention to those around them. We'll look at the whole issue of etiquette afloat in detail on pages 62–63, but in the meantime, consider the following:

• Don't set out on your own unless you know exactly what you're doing.

• Don't assume, because you can sail from one side of the lake to the other in good weather, that you're ready to set off into the open sea.
• Don't go anywhere too out of the way until you're confident you can cope; and check to see if there's a rescue boat on call.
• Always tell someone where you're going (be very specific about it) and when you expect to be back. Arrange a time to call them on your return; that way they will know to contact the emergency services

on your behalf, and they can actually provide useful information to the search party. Telling someone that you're "off out for the day" doesn't count.
• Always get a weather forecast before you set out, so that you're prepared for inconveniences (like a heavy downpour) and can avoid major problems (like an incoming storm). Never take chances; never overestimate your own skills.
• Don't go out after sunset unless you know what you're doing and have good lights.
• Always give yourself plenty of time to get back to shore. It's better to arrive early than find yourself having to rush back—that's when you make mistakes.
• If you're in an estuary or making your way out to sea, make sure you consult the local tide table and charts; the mouths of estuaries in particular are fickle places and the currents can be hard to predict.
• If you're going out at low tide and anticipate returning at high, note any obstacles that may be under the water when you come back.
• Sailboat captains should always be on the lookout for overhead pylons; these will zap you and your boat if they touch the mast.

Always be considerate of other water users, particularly on crowded lakes or if they're clearly inexperienced.

- Commercial shipping lanes are for big ships and not for you; stay well away.
- Even if it's calm on the shoreline, the offshore winds can be much stronger and powerful enough to confound even an experienced sailor. Be prepared, or they may prove more than you can handle.
- Sometimes local regulations will restrict the distance from the shore you're allowed to go, depending on the size of your boat; make sure you know what these restrictions are and that you follow them.
- Learn the "rules of the road"—see pages 58–61— and refresh your memory before casting off.
- Make sure you drink plenty of water when you're on board.
- If you get very cold and wet, consider returning early; the effects of a chill wind on a wet body can be profound and cause serious problems.
- Don't go out if you're feeling unwell; being in a boat will make you feel worse rather than better, and your judgment will be impaired.
- Take extra care if there are larger, faster vessels about, especially if you're in something that sits low in the water and may not be seen at distance; remember that not all water users are necessarily as conscientious as you are.
- Make sure you complete the pre-cast-off safety check (see page 50) before you leave.

Carry a Spare

If you wear eyeglasses and need them for close or distance work, here's some advice. Buy one of those straps to hook round the arms so they dangle from your neck (the glasses, not your arms). You may look like grandma, but you'll be grateful when you don't sit on them or they don't fly overboard because you did something stupid which threatened to knock them off your head. And carry a spare pair of eyeglasses in a case that floats—all such cases on a boat should float—and keep them somewhere safe where you can find them easily. It's no fun trying to run a boat when you can't see what you're doing—especially when the time comes to return to dock, or judge the moment to jump out before dragging the boat up the shore.

Vessel Safety Check

A vessel safety check is a straightforward procedure that, in many territories, costs nothing. It's a bow-to-stern examination of your boat by a suitably qualified inspector—typically a member of the Coast Guard or another approved examiner—and is the easiest way to highlight any potential problems with a boat that's been bought second-hand or hasn't been used for a while. Remember that it's up to you to ascertain whether or not your boat meets the standards that may be required by law in your particular territory. A vessel safety check will help you to do this.

Here is a comprehensive run-down of things that will need to be checked, based on what the US Coast Guard requires. Not all of these will apply to you; it depends on the kind of boat you use, where you take it out, and where you live. Still, when it comes to safety, it's best to start at the top and work down; remember that some insurers offer discounts if your boat has passed a vessel safety check.

• **State and/or Local Requirements**
Before you can pass the safety check, you must fulfill any legal requirements appropriate for your area.

• **Display of Numbers**
The registration number needs to be displayed permanently on the forward part of the boat on each side. The color must contrast well against the background; the characters must be 3 in tall (or greater); the letters and numbers must be separated clearly by a hyphen or a space.

• **Registration and Documentation**
If the boat displaces more than 5 tons, then

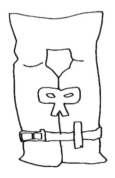

Three different styles of life jacket

registration documents must be held on board and the number displayed prominently on the boat's structure. The boat's name and hailing port (the port to which it is registered) must also be displayed on the exterior hull, using characters of 4 in or taller.

• **Personal Flotation Devices (PFDs)**
You'll need one life jacket per person on the boat, and they must fit properly; an adult's PFD will not be suitable for a kid. They must be easily accessible and immediately available for use—not still in the plastic bag that they came in. Boats of more than 16 ft must have at least one Type IV PFD; this is a device that can be thrown to someone in the water, who can grab onto it—it is not designed to be worn.

• **Visual Distress Signals (VDSs)**
The requirement here varies depending on whether the boat's being used on coastal or inland waters, and during the day or night. You should have at least one day and one night pyrotechnic device and maybe some

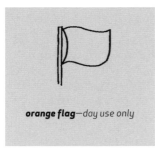

orange flag—day use only

red distress flare (handheld)—day and night use (minimum of three required)

flashlight—night use only

arm signals (wear bright clothing)

orange smoke signal (handheld)—day use only (minimum of three required)

orange smoke signal (floating)—day use only (minimum of three required)

alternatives; for example, a strobe light, signal mirror, flashlight, lantern, or red and orange flags.

• **Fire Extinguishers**
You'll need these if you've got an inboard engine, closed compartments that contain portable fuel tanks, a double-bottom hull that isn't completely sealed or filled with flotation materials, an enclosed living space, closed compartments that store anything that can burn, or fuel tanks. A pre-cast-off check of the boat should be carried out to ascertain that the extinguishers are easy to get at, and work properly. There are different requirements regarding the number of fire extinguishers, depending on the boat's length.

• **Ventilation**
If you've got a gasoline engine in a closed compartment, you'll need

red meteor—day or night (minimum of three required)

Above are the various options available for visual distress signals, and whether they are suitable for day and/or night use.

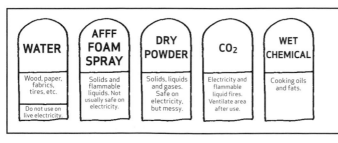

WATER	AFFF FOAM SPRAY	DRY POWDER	CO₂	WET CHEMICAL
Wood, paper, fabrics, tires, etc.	Solids and flammable liquids. Not usually safe on electricity.	Solids, liquids and gases. Safe on electricity, but messy.	Electricity and flammable liquid fires. Ventilate area after use.	Cooking oils and fats.
Do not use on live electricity.				

Remember that specific extinguishers—water, foam spray, dry powder, CO_2, and wet chemical—are required to tackle different kinds of fire.

Vessel Safety Check continued

either natural or powered ventilation, depending on the age of the boat.

• Backfire Flame Control
If you've got a gas-powered inboard or outboard motor, it must have an approved backfire flame control device to disperse the backfire into the atmosphere and reduce the danger of an explosion or open fire.

• Sound-Producing Devices
You need something like a whistle, siren, or horn capable of making a four-second blast that can be heard half a mile away. Boats longer than 16 ft are also required to have a bell.

• Navigation Lights
You're expected to display navigation lights between sunset and sunrise, or during daylight hours if the

conditions warrant it—for example, in fog. Boats longer than 16 ft must have navigation lights and an all-round anchor light that operates independently of any running lights.

• Pollution Placard
In many regions, boats over 26 ft that have a machinery compartment need to have a placard proclaiming that they're giving off oily waste.

• MARPOL Trash Placard
Longer boats need to display one of these (the name is short for "marine pollution"); larger boats may need to display a written garbage disposal plan.

• Marine Sanitation Devices
If you have a toilet, it

must be an approved device and you must be able to seal any outlets to prevent discharge if required.

• Navigation Rules
You should also have a copy of the current rules of navigation.

• Overall Vessel Condition
The deck should be clear and hazard-free, there should be no obvious fire hazards, and the bilges should be reasonably clean. The inspector will also make a visual check to see if the hull is sound. Both the fuel and electrical systems will need a check. The electrical system should be fused, or use circuit breakers which can be manually reset. Fuses and switches must be covered properly to protect them from spray damage, and there should be no exposed wiring at all. Batteries must be secured properly and their terminals

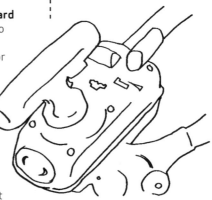

How Long Does an Inspection Take?

This depends on the size of the boat, but typically about 20 minutes. The examiner will check approximately 15 items on the boat and then talk to you about other safety issues, answer any questions you may have, and so on. At the end—assuming you've passed—you'll get a copy of the form and a VSC decal to display, showing that your boat comes up to scratch.

Didn't I Get One of These when I Bought the Boat?

That's a marine survey, which is something different. Sure, it covers many of the same things, but it's mainly to satisfy the finance company that the asking price for the boat is a fair one and that there's nothing catastrophically wrong with it. A vessel safety check is part of the ongoing "life" of your boat. Things change every day, and over the course of a season or two it's best to make sure that your boat still meets the same high standards that it did when you first bought it.

protected to prevent dangerous arcing; all personal watercraft require a "kill-switch" mechanism. Portable fuel tanks must be free of corrosion and leaks, and made of non-breakable material, with vapor-proof caps; they must also be secured. All permanent tanks must be ventilated properly. So far as the galley and any heating systems are concerned, they must be properly secured and the area clear of any and all flammable material.

When Should I Wear a PFD?

Some places have legislation covering this, so just check the regulations before you go. Otherwise, you should wear a PFD if there are lots of other boats about, if the weather conditions are poor, if the water conditions are uncomfortable, if you're a long way from shore, if it's dark or there is low visibility, or if you're alone on the boat. In fact, any time you feel like you should be wearing your PFD, you should put it on—it's much harder to get into one on a rocking boat, or worse still, in the water, than in calm and unhurried conditions.

Provisioning the Galley

There are two basic ways to put a galley kitchen together. First, you can spend a lot of money buying and fitting (or getting someone else to fit) various boat-friendly specialized devices and gizmos. Second, you can make do with stuff you've got at home or that you pick up second-hand at yard sales. We follow the school of thought that says anything cooked in a galley kitchen tastes ten times better than the same thing cooked on dry land—and if that's the case, then think how great it is to prepare it using cookware that cost little or nothing to buy. Perhaps inevitably, we're going to recommend the middle way: there are certain gizmos that you should buy and others that are unnecessary.

Must-Haves

- Everything moves around on a boat—everything. Invest in plastic or lightweight metal dishes and utensils; some people hate them, but acrylic glasses are a much better bet than ones made out of real glass.
- Get one of those grills that hook on the railing of a boat and can be used for barbecues.
- Look for a cutting board that clips onto something else for stability, or choose one that folds down from the galley wall to create a dedicated area for food preparation; make sure that it's easy to clean and comes off the wall once a year for a scrub-down.

Alternatively, you can buy cutting boards that fit over the top of the stove, though these are expensive.
- Buy a magnetized strip to temporarily store any knives you're using for food prep, then clean and put them away safely when you've finished. Remember what we said about everything moving around?
- As for the galley, look for safety rails that you can grab onto—boats move, even when they're in dock.

What Kind of Stove?

If you have a large boat and cruise all year round, then you can use a diesel stove, which will deliver the kind of quality normally associated with a landbound stove and keep the boat warm in winter as well. Needs to be a big boat, though, because it's heavy. If you're often out for days at a time, then gas is the most convenient, and is still relatively inexpensive. For day trips or shorter, consider a spirit stove; if you find the smell a problem (some do, many don't), try diluting the fuel with about 10 percent water and it should disappear completely.

Why the "Head"?

It's like this. Originally, "head" referred to the front of the boat, which was where, on older ships, sailors would go to relieve themselves. Standing on a grate, they were able to take advantage of the sea's natural flushing properties, which also washed over the grate, keeping the area clean. The name stuck.

- Cupboards should have safety latches, and these need checking periodically.
- Avoid expensive boating stores unless they carry something you can't get elsewhere; camping stores usually carry equivalent goods at lower prices.

- Get a large cooler—one big enough and strong enough to sit on. It provides an extra seat and is useful extra storage for those items that can't fit in the refrigerator, either because it's not big enough or because you haven't got one.

- Make sure that you remember to bring a few good basic utensils as well: for example, a couple of spatulas, a selection of wooden spoons, two can openers, two bottle openers (see a pattern emerging here?), and a camping kettle.

In Praise of the Pressure Cooker

If you're cooking on a boat, then treat yourself to a pressure cooker, which, along with the wok and the Dutch oven, is probably the world's most versatile cooking pot. It's not really any good for roasting or any kind of frying, but it's great for almost everything else, because the pressure of the steam cooks things much more quickly. A pot of potatoes will cook in about 5 minutes, a whole chicken in about 20 minutes! Pressure cookers are space-saving, use less fuel, they kill more germs because food is cooked beyond the point at which water normally boils, they lock more goodness in, they're easy to use and clean, and are great either for one-pot meals or for cooking several things at once.

Clothing

There's nothing quite so smart as a well turned-out sailor—no, seriously. Look, they know exactly what they look like, but there's a method in that sartorial madness and it's this: if you don't keep warm and dry on a boat, your concentration starts to go, and you can quickly put yourself and anyone else on the boat in danger.

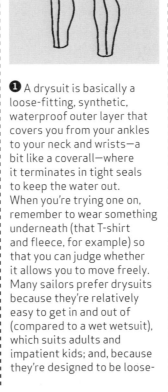

Those engaged in the more sedate forms of sailing may generally wear what they like. Since you're outdoors, you should wear layers—for example, a cotton T-shirt and a microfleece or woolen shirt, and have a thin, breathable waterproof on top—this is the most effective way of keeping warm. Otherwise, you just need shoes with a good grip, that won't mark the deck. If it's a fancy boat, you may want to consult the skipper about what they consider to be suitable.

If conditions warrant more protection, then there are two main options open to you: a drysuit and a wetsuit.

❶ A drysuit is basically a loose-fitting, synthetic, waterproof outer layer that covers you from your ankles to your neck and wrists—a bit like a coverall—where it terminates in tight seals to keep the water out. When you're trying one on, remember to wear something underneath (that T-shirt and fleece, for example) so that you can judge whether it allows you to move freely. Many sailors prefer drysuits because they're relatively easy to get in and out of (compared to a wet wetsuit), which suits adults and impatient kids; and, because they're designed to be loose-

fitting, even the fastest-growing kid will get several years' wear out of one. Look for a diagonal front zipper rather than the old-fashioned zipper across the shoulders, so you can undo it yourself without any help. Check that the backside and knees are properly reinforced, as these get the most wear and tear.

❷ A wetsuit is also a good choice for a wide range of conditions (apart from when it's super-hot), and works by trapping a layer of water between the suit and your skin, which then heats it to body temperature; this keeps you warm. It's therefore important that the suit fits snugly and doesn't allow fresh water to get in and circulate, because that will just make you cold. Look for knee pads, and when trying it on, bend and stretch to make sure it fits properly.

Both kinds of suit are expensive and need a little care. Wash them with fresh water after use, then hang them to dry on a plastic hanger out of direct sunlight. A little talcum powder on the seals will make them easier to pull on and off, and a bit of candle wax will help to keep the zipper running smoothly.

Activities Checklist

There's more to being on a boat than just being on a boat. There's the stuff of running the boat to do of course, but there's also the stuff that's fun to do, or interesting, or even—dare we say it—educational. In Section Six we'll be suggesting some activities that all ages can enjoy, and on this page we've put together a checklist of items that you'll need to pull it off. If you need more detail about any of the items here, turn to the relevant pages to find out more.

- **Waterside Attractions (page 92):** decent walking shoes, simple rain gear, beach stuff (towel, sunscreen, hat, sunglasses, inflatable toys for kids, and so on); maps for nearby attractions, walks, bike paths, and campsites.

- **Aquatic Scavenger Hunt (page 93):** a big set of pens, pencils, crayons, felt-tips, and paper; ring-bound books for keeping a log; a reference book of plants and animals that live in or near sea and fresh water, to help you come up with things for people to find.

- **Semaphore Flag Code (page 94):** pairs of flags, either store-bought or made from red and yellow card.

- **Castaway for a Day (page 95):** a tent and sleeping bags, and maybe some camping

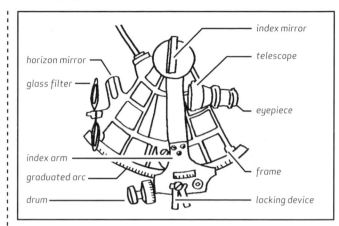

mattresses; torches, fire-lighting gear, hurricane-style lamp, knife, rope and string, food to cook, mobile phone or walkie-talkie.

- **Supervised Activities (pages 96–7):** money to pay for them!

- **Fishing (pages 98–9):** rods, fixed-spool reels, line, and end tackle; bait; also, hand lines and nets.

- **Watching Wildlife (pages 100–1):** binoculars, reference books.

- **Measuring Wind Speed (page 102):** plastic cups, a large felt-tipped pen, phone or walkie-talkie, stapler, ruler, thumbtacks,

scissors, pencil with an eraser, two cardboard strips, and a watch with a second hand.

- **Making a Telescope (page 103):** cardboard tube, convex lenses of different focal lengths, sticky tape.

- **Swimming (pages 104–5):** snorkels and masks, flippers, inflatables, underwater camera or case.

- **Ghost Stories, Sea Shanties, and Games (pages 106–7):** your imagination..

- **Celestial Navigation (pages 108–9):** the telescope shown on page 103 (or, if it didn't work, binoculars); alternatively, a cardboard sextant (see above)!

Pre-Cast-Off Checklist

Although it may seem as though we've gone checklist crazy, it's important to make sure that the boat and the people on it are prepared for as many eventualities as possible. The checklist is a valuable tool, especially as there's usually a rush to get on the boat and get going, and it can help to ensure that you don't forget anything important.

with particular reference to watching the weather, docking and undocking, what to do in the case of a mechanical emergency, and what to do if a person falls overboard.
• If you've refueled, open your hatches, run your blower, and check for fumes before firing up the engine.

If the boat has regular vessel safety checks (see pages 42–5), the skipper can do a quick, "light" version of that, then add a check of supplies such as fuel, oil, and water; also check that the bilges are dry and the pumps aren't running too hard. Then work your way through the following, especially if you have others on board who aren't used to being on a boat:

• Check the weather forecast.
• Make sure you have a radio on board with which you can check weather updates.
• Make sure that everyone knows where the personal flotation devices (PFDs) are and how to put them on. Make sure that each person knows which is theirs, so two people don't reach for the same one.
• Make sure everyone knows where the fire extinguishers are and how to use them.
• Then do the same with the flares and sound-producing devices.
  • Demonstrate the use of the radio and what to do in an emergency.
  • Show everyone the anchor, explain how it works and when to use it.
• Explain the responsibilities of everyone on the boat

Float Plan

Although not necessarily a legal requirement, it's always a good idea to prepare one and give it to someone responsible to look after. The plan outlines your itinerary (include stop-offs as well as your eventual destination) and includes not just a description of the boat but also your name and address, the boat name and any relevant registration numbers, the number of people on board, and instructions on who to contact should you not check in at the time you're supposed to.

First-Aid Kit

Most boating trips go off without a hitch, but common sense—and, in some regions, legal requirements—dictates that you must be prepared for those times when things don't go according to plan. A first-aid kit is therefore one of the most important items you'll be packing for your trip, whether it's long or short, adventurous or simply relaxing.

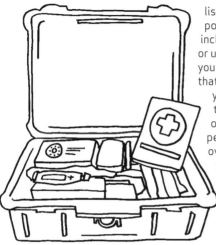

list here as a starting point. If the kit you buy includes fancy equipment or utilizes techniques that you don't understand or that are clearly beyond your capabilities, then there's no point. One of the biggest mistakes people make is to worry over those situations that clearly require trained medical staff—your job then is to make the injured person as comfortable as possible and seek assistance as soon as you can.

We'll look at some specific first-aid techniques on pages 126–130, but in the meantime, here is a good starting point if you're putting together your own medical kit:

Most medical situations on a boat are similar to their shorebound counterparts. In other words, they're inconveniences that are at worst a little uncomfortable. The discomfort may be exacerbated if you're a long way out from the shore, but it should be something you can deal with effectively. Thus, to go along with the medical kit listed on this page, you also need some knowledge—so either get yourself a decent medical manual or, better still, go on a recognized first-aid course. Best of all, do both.

Many specialist suppliers will be happy to sell you a ready-made first-aid kit for your boat, but use the

- First-aid tape, a couple of 3 in elastic bandage rolls, 10 sterile gauze pads, half a dozen "butterfly" closure strips, two 9x5 in trauma pads, a triangular bandage.
- Sunburn cream or sunblock, antiseptic cream, hydrocortisone cream, lip balm, insect repellent.
- Aspirin, ibuprofen, an antihistamine, laxatives, medication for diarrhea.
- A packet of disposable surgical gloves, antiseptic cleaning wipes, different sizes of safety pins, tweezers, a scalpel, a pair of small, tough scissors, EMT surgical shears, CPR shield/mask, a thermometer.

Known Medical Conditions

If anyone on your boat has a specific medical condition, they should have a physical beforehand to ensure that they're able to sail in the first place. If they're passed OK, it's up to them to make sure they bring any medication they need and that everyone else on the trip is aware of their condition in case anything should happen. Sailing is a hobby that can be enjoyed by all, and if you take due care there's no reason why you shouldn't be able to keep at it well into your later years.

SECTION FOUR

Basic Navigation

Launching the Boat

Seasoned sailors make the comparison with taking off in a plane—it's the most difficult bit about learning to fly. It can be a bit nerve-wracking, especially for the first few times, or if you're going solo. It can also feel pressured, especially if you're trying to launch in a busy harbor or move out of a crowded marina where there's an audience, but there are certain procedures that will make life a bit easier. As for "landing" your boat, we'll cover that on pages 68–69.

There are so many different kinds of boats and so many different environments in which to use them that it's difficult to generalize about situations you might come across. However, the most common situations can be broken down as follows:

• **Launching from the Shore**
If you're renting a small boat or canoe, the owners will usually have found a favorable spot for hauling them in and out. If you're arriving at a strange place, choose somewhere clear of rocks and other obstructions, and not overrun by other water users. If it's tidal, try and talk to someone to make sure that the gently sloping beach doesn't turn into steep shingle at high tide, or you may not be able to get back out. If you're carrying a small boat to the water, take care not to knock the bottom against the ground—boats are obviously at their most vulnerable when they're out of the water like this.

Using a lightweight trailer that you can wheel into the water makes the most sense—though if you're on your own you may have to ask for help. Most water users are obliging, though they will need to be told what to do.

• **Launching from a Ramp (or Slipway)**
First, practice reversing your vehicle and trailer so you don't find yourself in the position of trying to do it for the first time in a strange place in front of a curious crowd. Second, try and make sure the ramp or slipway you intend to use is suitable for your boat—not just whether it'll fit, but whether the water

is tidal. When you arrive at a new slipway, don't just back straight down, but look out for anything unusual that you may not have experienced before—every slipway has its quirks. Walk up and down it to see if it's muddy or slippery. If you're able to find someone in charge (beyond the person who takes the money), ask their advice; remember that a slipway may be too steep or plain awkward for a car, in which case the trailer needs to go down on its own at the end of a rope. If they offer assisted launching and you're the uncertain type, take them up on it; you may end up needing extra help anyway. There are too many types of trailers to go into specifics here; just make sure always to launch your boat in the way that is safe for you, for everyone else, for your boat, and for your vehicle.

• **Leaving a Mooring** (or a quay or pontoon)
You'll need to know about the ropes, cleats, and lashings (that's "knots" to the rest of

Leaving and returning to a mooring takes practice, so be prepared for a few early mishaps.

us) that are used to moor your boat, and how to undo them in the correct order. If you're side-on, you'll release these ropes stern-first or bow-first, depending on the wind conditions, and you may also have what are called "springs," which help to stop the bow or stern of the boat swinging out. A swinging mooring is a different kettle of fish: the

boat is only attached by a single line, but care needs to be taken to ensure that you don't foul the mooring line as you move off. On lakes you may be moored up by the bow (bows-on) or the stern (stern-on), in which case the procedure is different. Stern-on makes it easier to get from the quay onto the boat, but also means you have to be confident reversing in—and that's a real skill. Always let the boat owners either side of you know when you're preparing to leave a mooring—it's both good practice and courteous.

Planning Ahead
You can usually find information about a launch site ahead of time by telephoning or checking the Internet. Alternatively, it's often possible to find printed publications which can help you out. In small countries you may find annually updated catalogs with comprehensive lists of where to go and what to expect when you get there. In larger territories, these publications usually offer regional or state-wide coverage. Expect information on charges, type of ramp, access, facilities, hazards, tides, and speed limits.

Moving Off

So, the boat's in the water and you're in the boat—what's next? Well, now you have to get it to go somewhere, preferably in the direction you want, in a controlled fashion, and without hitting anything or anybody else. There are so many variations involved in moving that it's impossible to cover them all. The idea here, then, is to give you a couple of examples of situations that may arise.

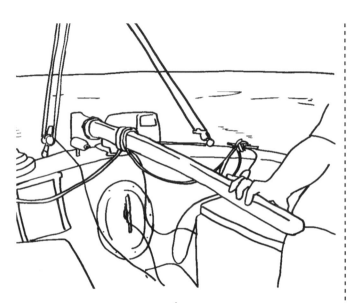

Think About Other People

Watch carefully for other water users, especially those that may be actually in the water and therefore harder to see. Well-run lakes and foreshores will separate swimming areas from boating ones, but at more occasional or out-of-the-way venues this may not be the case. Etiquette usually requires you to inform the people either side of your berth that you're planning to move off, and this will save tangles and misunderstandings. Always proceed with care, don't reverse out unless you know actually know how

to—it's probably one of the most difficult of boating skills—and maneuver using your engines, assuming that you have them, until you're away from people and other water craft.

Only once you're out of the marina or harbor and into open water should you raise your sails. If your boat has fenders—shock absorbers that can be lowered over the side of the boat to cushion the effect of hitting another boat or a dock, piling, quay, or whatever—be prepared to deploy them. There's so much to do and to watch out for when you're setting off in a boat of any size, that it's

always a great deal easier if there's more than one person running things.

The Tiller Works Back to Front!

One of the main differences between steering a car and skippering a boat is that, while a boat's wheel works the same as a steering wheel in a car—spin it right to turn right—a tiller works in exactly the opposite way. So, move the tiller to the right and the boat goes left, move it to the left and it turns right. Though this is not exactly a complicated concept to get your head around, it's easy to forget under pressure and think that you're still driving a car. By the way, when you're moving off slowly, you'll have to turn harder and hold it for longer to get the kind of control you want. When you're able to pick up speed you should find that a lighter hand on the tiller will produce the same results.

The Wind in Your Favor

In a perfect situation, you're moored side-on and the wind is pushing your boat away from the dock. Start your engine first, but leave it in neutral; this gives you some control in case everything else goes wrong, and also

How to Get Into a Canoe

To avoid comedy canoe capers when getting into your canoe, try this. Get on sideways. Take the arm nearest to the canoe and use it to hold the top of the side nearest to you. Step into the boat with the leg that's also nearest to the canoe. Transfer the first arm across so it's holding the other side, and grasp the first side with your other arm. Still holding both sides of the canoe, step into the boat with your other leg. Try and keep your center of gravity low when you're in a canoe, and move slowly. Try and board so that you're already in your paddling position. If you can (some people find it uncomfortable), kneel in a canoe to achieve maximum stability.

The Wind Against You

Should the wind be pushing you into the dock, then cast off any lines except one securing the bow. Use the rudder/tiller/wheel to push the stern out from the dock, and then release the front line and reverse very slowly away from the dock and out into more open water. Slow, and then turn the boat away from the dock, moving forward slowly.

ensures that you know the engine will actually start. Cast off the lines, pull up the fenders, and let the wind do its job. When you're far enough away from the quay, start engines and move off slowly. Make sure you leave enough room between you and the quay before you start, otherwise the boat may pivot and the stern will smack into the quay. The first few times that you try this, it might be a good idea to have someone standing by to drop a fender over the side and absorb the force of the impact.

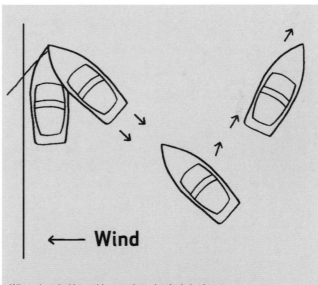

When the wind is pushing you into the dock, let loose all but the bow line. Maneuver the stern out from the dock, let go the bow line, and reverse out slowly. Turn the bow away from the dock and move off.

Rules of the Road

Just like dry land, there are rules that govern what happens when two vehicles (in this case boats) get close to each other. So long as both know how to navigate around the other properly, and who has right of way in a specific situation, then there's no danger of a collision—certainly less danger than there is when you're driving along the road. There are essentially two different sets of rules that govern the way boats interact with each other, on inland and international waters. Your chart will indicate clearly when you're moving from one to the other and, thus, when you need to make the mental switch.

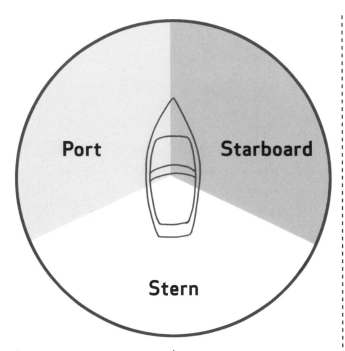

Powered vessels must give way to:
- vessels under oars, such as canoes or kayaks;
- sailboats that are under sail (sailboats that are running on their engines count as powered vessels);
- commercial fishing vessels which are unable to maneuver quickly (this excludes sports fishing boats);
- big, slow vessels, such as dredgers, boats that are towing other boats, boats that are restricted to a particular area because of the work they're doing or because of their draft;
- vessels that have broken down, and are thus "not under command."

Since most beginners are going to be doing their boating on the inland side of the demarcation line, that's what we'll be concentrating on. A couple of bits of jargon before we start: the boat which has the right of way and is thus supposed to keep its course and speed is usually known as the "stand-on" vessel; the one that changes course is usually known as the "give-way" vessel.

There's a hierarchy on the water that's based on maneuverability, and it goes like this:

- Power-driven vessels are at the top of this tree because they're the most maneuverable and—because they're engine-driven—the least affected by the weather. (Even the fastest sailboat won't go anywhere without the wind.)

So, for example, a yacht must give way to, or avoid, a commercial fishing boat, while a fishing boat must give way to a dredger. The potential problems arise when two similar vessels approach each other, and that's when the following collision rules come into action. First, let's briefly recap what we learned on page 30. Imagine you're standing on a boat, facing

Very Big Boats

The safest course of action is to stay away from them. They are cumbersome to maneuver, and when they turn on the brakes it can take them up to one mile before they actually stop. If you see a tug and then a barge some way behind it, don't think you can squeeze through the gap—there may be a gap, but there may also be a submerged cable between them that you can't see. All large ships have a blind spot that can extend for a considerable distance; this won't matter if you steer clear of them. Very large ships may act as windbreaks, decreasing your speed and making it difficult for you to maneuver; they also create a large wake which can make life very uncomfortable if you are in a small boat.

If another powered vessel approaches your port side, stick to the same course and proceed cautiously.

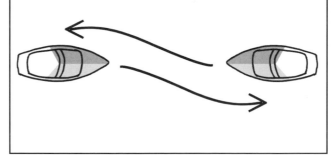

If you're about to meet another powered vessel head on, sound your horn and then alter course to starboard.

forward. The port side is on your left, the starboard on your right, and anything behind is astern.

When Two Motorboats Meet

• If two motorboats approach head-on, then one must issue a single short blast on its sound-producing device and then alter course to starboard so that the two boats pass on the port side.

If the wind is blowing thus, the vessel which is receiving wind on its port side must take action to avoid the vessel receiving wind on the starboard side.

Wind

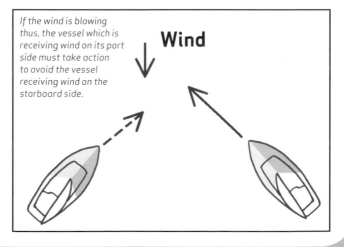

SECTION FOUR

Rules of the Road continued

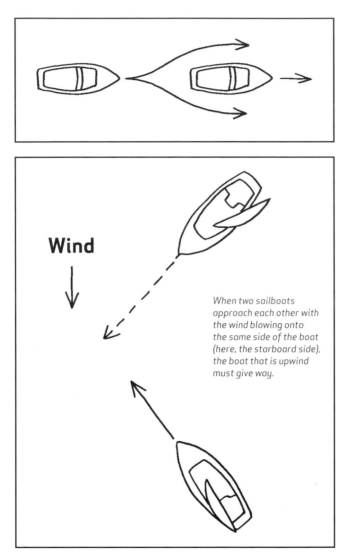

Wind

When two sailboats approach each other with the wind blowing onto the same side of the boat (here, the starboard side), the boat that is upwind must give way.

• If another motorboat comes up on your port side, you should maintain your course—it's up to the other boat to avoid you. But be ready to move off to starboard if it becomes clear that they don't intend to change course.

• If another motorboat approaches from your starboard side, then you must get out of their way by altering your course and speed.

• If a second motorboat approaches from your stern (see top left), you may continue to proceed at your present speed. It's up to the boat behind to overtake you, allowing plenty of space; boats can overtake on either the port or starboard sides. Until the overtaking boat is completely clear of the other, it is the give-way vessel and must act accordingly.

When Two Sailboats Meet

This is a little different, because the wind direction determines who does what. In brief, you establish who has right of way by working out which side of the boat the wind is blowing into—this is called the windward side, remember.

• For example, imagine one boat at 9 o'clock and the other at 3 o'clock, both sailing north toward 12 o'clock and into the wind. The boat with the wind blowing into its port side

Fast Rivers

If you're enjoying yourself on fast-running water, there's a general and obvious rule: if two boats meet in a channel, the one going downstream has right of way. This is because it's much harder to stop yourself and give way when the current is with you than it is to hold your position against the current until the other boat has passed downstream of you.

must avoid the other boat by taking prompt and definite evasive action.

- Alternatively, suppose both boats have the wind blowing onto the same side—let's say they're at 2 o'clock and 5 o'clock, sailing toward the center of the clock face, and the wind is blowing from 12 o'clock. The 2 o'clock boat must give way to the other boat because, although both are "receiving" wind on their starboard sides, the 2 o'clock boat is upwind (i.e. closer to the direction the wind is blowing from) of the other one.

After You

There are certain situations when it's really not clear who should make the first move. You can solve this problem by always being the person who decides first. Make it your business to stay out of other people's way, and you won't go far wrong. The only problem with this is that too many sailors don't take action early enough or definitely enough, so that the second skipper doesn't understand what they're trying to do. The answer is to make your move early and with definite purpose—that way your intentions will be clear.

Audible Signals

When it's not easy for two skippers to see each other—for example, when one wants to overtake another—there are various audible signals that can be used to indicate what you want to do. Confusingly, these signals vary, depending on where you are.

The good news is that in international waters the signals are always the same. If you're heading in the same direction as another boat and you want to overtake them on their port side, you should give two long blasts and two short blasts on your horn; if they agree, they'll respond with one long, followed by one short. To overtake on the starboard side, you'd issue two long, followed by one short, and they'd reply with one long, one short, one long, and one short.

On inland waters, however, things are different. In the US, for example, the same scenario would go like this. If you want to overtake someone on their port side, you issue two short, one-second blasts on the horn; if the boat ahead answers with two similar blasts, then you know it's OK to proceed. To overtake on their starboard side, you'd issue a single one-second blast and they'd answer with the same.

It's obviously important to know the specific rules that apply in the region you're sailing, so make sure you find out what they are and stick to them.

Always give way to commercial fishing vessels. They can't maneuver as easily as you and it's therefore your job to avoid them.

Etiquette Afloat

Being on board a boat for the first time is great fun, but it's challenging too. In such a relatively confined space, it's important that everyone is able to rub along together and get on. One of the ways to make sure this happens is to be aware that the rules for life on board are different from those on land. Here are some of the key ones.

Manners at the Marina

- If there's no one around to assist another boat as it's docking or undocking, offer to help—it makes you part of the sailing community.
- "Own" the area around your mooring and make sure it's clear of obstacles. Carefully stow those loose hoses and lines, and make sure there are no cables to trip up a passerby who may be less able than you, or shortsighted, or just not looking where they're going.

Make sure you do the same with buckets, mops, and other cleaning gear.

- If you're using communal equipment that belongs to the marina, remember it's intended for everyone—not just you—so put it back where it came from, so that it doesn't make the place look untidy, and so that others can use it.
- Stopping for fuel should be just that. Other people want to fill up too, so don't tie up there and then wander off to

check out the marina's gym or go shopping. Follow the instructions to fill up, pay the person, and then move off to a more appropriate part of the marina where you can tie up.

- Join the queue for fuel; it may not be obvious, but that boat idling over there may be waiting in a line that you're not yet aware of—push in front of them, and you soon will be!
- If it's hot and you like to take advantage of your air-conditioning—which means running the generator all night—try to find a quiet spot away from other people who may not appreciate its constant hum.
- If your boat is more like a recreational vehicle (there's nothing wrong with that) and is wired to the gunwales with a state-of-the-art stereo, a pair of teenage kids, and all their friends, move even further away.
- Off out for the night? Make sure you turn off your VHF radio, your instruments, and any outside lights. If the marina is poorly lit, then you can keep a soft light burning in the cabin.

As a rule of thumb, you can tell the depth of the water by its color. Some people find a simple rhyme helps them to remember:

Brown brown, run aground.

White, white, then you might.

Green, green, nice and clean.

Blue, blue, sail on through.

Catchy, huh?

Anchoring Etiquette

We're not going to get into how to anchor here, because it's a complicated subject, but we will venture the following, because it affects lots of sailors who like to travel further and maybe lay up overnight.

- The general rule is that whoever arrives first at an anchorage sets the style; in other words, the first couple of boats will determine where you anchor, how much distance you leave between you and the next boat, and so on. The only exception is if you believe that someone has anchored incorrectly given the conditions; in this case you should make your own judgment based on how safe the anchorage is, and how easy it is to leave quickly and safely should you need to.

- You should always examine an anchorage first, rather than just charging straight in—and don't hesitate to ask for advice or help from people who are already there and may have done the work for you. Remember to check on your likely neighbors; if you want peace and quiet, move away from them, or find somewhere else entirely.

- Come in slowly; don't upset your new neighbors by knocking their dinner drinks over, courtesy of the wake you just created.

- Sound travels further over water, so bear that in mind, whether you're partying or just talking on your cell phone; cigarette smoke can travel a long way downwind as well.

- If you're already anchored and someone else arrives, don't be afraid to tell them if they're getting too close.

- If your anchor starts to drag, take the decision early to up anchor and move somewhere with a better grip; don't wait until you're nearly whacking into the boat next door before you do something about it.

Navigational Aids and Aids to Navigation

Not the pedantic hairsplitting it seems to be, but rather the difference between those devices which are on your boat which help you work out which way to go, and those outside your boat which do the same thing. The key, as always, is to get where you want to go safely, without getting lost, or bumping into anyone or anything else.

Navigational Aids

The most important are **maps and charts** of various kinds. On a canal boat or small pleasure cruiser, you'll probably be able to get by with the equivalent of a map from the local tourist office which will show routes, locks, moorings, tie-ups, and other important features of the various types of inland waters. If you're traveling further afield in, say, a kayak, then a proper **topological map** will probably be most useful, partly because you'll usually be stopping off on the way to make camp or rest, and partly because there may well not be a detailed chart available for the river or lake, or lake system, itself. Topological maps are also useful for sailors in areas where no nautical charts exist, because they provide valuable information about the coastal landscape and indicate places where it may be possible, for example, to land a boat—or, perhaps even more importantly, where it's impossible to land a boat.

If you're planning to spend any time on a large body of water, or sailing around the coast or heading offshore, then you need a **nautical chart**, which will provide you with a graphical picture of the marine environment. These charts show the coastline, water depth, and characteristics of the sea, estuary, river, and lake bottom, as well as potential dangers and hazards, the location of man-made aids to navigation, and tidal information where appropriate. Nautical charts are updated on schedules that vary from 6 months right up to 12 years for very remote areas, so always check yours is up to date before you put your faith in it. A **marine compass** will help you to work out which way to go, and can be used to take bearings on aids to navigation (such as buoys) or natural landmarks. Once mastered, the compass is easy to use and maintain, reliable, and especially helpful in reduced visibility.

Although it's still important to learn the skills of map and compass reading, the life of the boating enthusiast has, like the lives of many car drivers, been transformed by **GPS**—the **Global Positioning System**. This is an electronic device that fixes your position by gathering information from a series of satellites orbiting the earth. Using it in conjunction with a paper chart, you can plot a course more accurately and more easily than ever before.

Aids to Navigation

The most common aid to navigation is a **buoy**—a floating marker, anchored to the bottom, used to indicate either a hazard or a safe passage. In Europe and Canada, for example, you'll find the **Cardinal System**, where buoys of particular colors and sizes are arranged in such a way as to show you the compass direction away from the hazard (see illustration, top right, opposite). The number of quick or very quick flashes relates to its position to the hazard; for example, three flashes means 3 o'clock, and therefore the eastward buoy.

Let Someone Else Do It for You

For the terminally disorganized, or just easily lost, there are plenty of guided or skippered options which you can use if you don't have a navigational bone in your body. These can range from fancy charters around the Caribbean or the Great Barrier Reef in Australia, where the emphasis is on luxury, right through to guided canoe tours through the Adirondack Mountains in New York State, where you'll work just as hard as your guide—except at reading maps or charts.

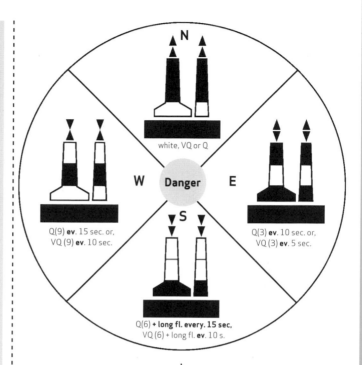

white, VQ or Q

W **Danger** **E**

Q(9) **ev**. 15 sec. or, VQ (9) **ev**. 10 sec.

Q(3) **ev**. 10 sec. or, VQ (3) **ev**. 5 sec.

Q(6) **+ long fl. every. 15 sec,** VQ (6) + long fl. **ev**. 10 s.

Then there's the **Lateral System**, where a series of red and green buoys indicates safe passage into a harbor, up a river, or out to sea. One color is used to indicate your port side and the other your starboard side, and by keeping to that you can follow the buoys safely into harbor or out to sea. Confusingly, however, the colors of the buoys are not always the same. For example, in the Americas, Philippines, Japan, and Korea, the port-side buoys are green and the starboard ones are red. If you're in Europe, Australasia, Asia, and parts of Africa, the port-side buoys will be red, and the starboard ones green. It's a bit like driving on the right in the US then remembering to drive on the left in England. You'll also come across other buoy types which indicate, for example, specific dangers, junctions, or a "fairway"—a safe stretch of water.

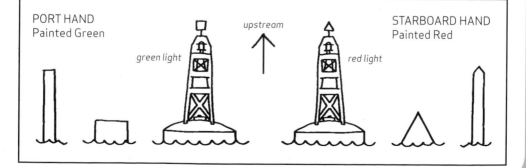

PORT HAND
Painted Green

green light

upstream

red light

STARBOARD HAND
Painted Red

Using Charts

Despite the fact that GPS technology allows accurate navigation with very little effort, you should always carry the fail-safe: a proper nautical chart, and anything else required to read it. Like reading any "serious" map—such as a topological map—this is a skill, but it actually doesn't take long to absorb it, and it's a satisfying skill to acquire.

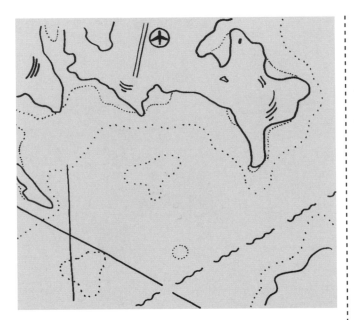

Nautical charts communicate a number of things:

• **Topography**
This is the physical landscape, the natural features, what are called "cultural features" (bridges, power lines, pipes, settlements, airports, and so on), landmarks (things that may be more easily visible, for example a church tower), different types of ports, and so on.

• **Hydrography**
This includes tides and currents, the depth, the physical characteristics of the sea bed, the positions of rocks, wrecks, and other underwater hazards, offshore installations like oil rigs, tracks and routes, along with areas and limits that may be open or closed to boats for various reasons.

• **Aids and Services**
These include lights (for example lighthouses), buoys, beacons, fog signals, electronic systems for fixing your position (for example radar and radio), services and facilities for small craft (for example a boarding place for a pilot, Coast Guard rescue station, lifeboat mooring, and so on).

They also have some important map "furniture" which helps you find your way around. For example, down the left- and right-hand sides of a map you'll find the **latitude** markings, and along the top and bottom you'll find the **longitude** markings. When used in conjunction with **parallel rules** (literally two rulers which are connected by small swinging arms), these help you to find your exact position on the map, based on your latitude and longitude. You'll also see sailors using a **plotter**, to work out their course, and **dividers** as a quick way to work out the distance between two points on the map. All of these devices have one thing in common: they're easy to use

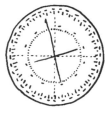

The compass rose helps you to tell the difference between degrees true and degrees magnetic.

SECTION FOUR

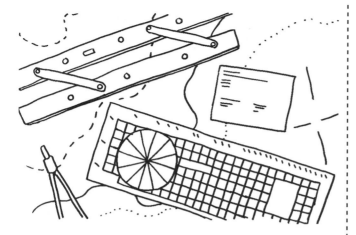

and display the result as a coordinate of latitude and longitude. The navigator can then use the nautical chart and instruments described above to find the exact position on the chart and mark it with a pencil.

Finally, although many of these skills and techniques will be most useful on a sea voyage, they're also important if you're on a large and unfamiliar inland water, or should visibility become significantly reduced, for example because of fog.

in an unsteady environment. Remember that boats move all the time, even when they're docked, and it's important to be able to hold any kind of measuring device in place easily; devices like these are designed to be quick and accurate under trying circumstances.

Depending on where you are in the world, your magnetic north changes relative to your true north (navigators generally, but not always, steer a course using magnetic north); in fact, if your chart covers a large enough area, it may change in the space of a single chart. That's when you'll need a **compass rose**, a visual representation of true and magnetic north that helps navigators work out which way to steer. Charts covering very large areas may have more than one compass rose.

We've mentioned **GPS** before, and these little devices have revolutionized navigation. Basically, you switch on your GPS and

it "talks" to a network of satellites orbiting the earth. The device is able to measure the distance between three or more of these satellites and itself by sending and receiving signals back and forth between them. Because it knows where each satellite is, and because these signals travel at a specific speed, the GPS device is able to work out exactly where it is relative to the satellites,

Dead Reckoning

This is a method of working out where you currently are, based on your last known position. For example, let's say you've been using your GPS to read off your position and marking it on the chart, and then the GPS stops working. Using your charts, compass, plotter, dividers, and parallel rules, you should be able to estimate where you are, based on your current speed and your current direction relative to magnetic north. It's not fantastically accurate, but it will give you a good approximation of where you are. This is another reason why it's so important to keep a logbook of where you are; the more recently you recorded your location, the more accurate your dead reckoning will be.

SECTION FOUR

Returning Safely

If moving away from the shore or mooring is like taking off in an airplane, then returning is exactly like landing. Combined, these are the two of most difficult things you'll ever do in a boat, but don't let that put you off. Here are a few tips for returning to where you came from with your boat, crew, and dignity intact.

The key to returning safely from whence you came is being able to control your speed—specifically, being able to slow down in a controlled fashion so that you can make the (occasionally quite fine) adjustments necessary to pick up a swinging mooring or just avoid banging into the dock, or other boats. If in doubt, err on the side of caution; and don't be afraid to make a few practice runs somewhere out of the way first, before you try your hand at a busy mooring or marina.

Returning to a Swinging Mooring
Broadly speaking, you should keep the following in mind on your return:

• If at all possible, try and approach your mooring heading into the wind, as this will help to slow down and eventually stop the boat.

• Check out the other boats already moored up, and see what direction they're facing—it's a good indication of the easiest way in.

• Pick up the floating rope next to the buoy with a boathook—that's what it's for, and it's a lot easier than trying to snag it by the handle, especially for a newbie.

• Keep pulling on the mooring rope until you reach the thicker rope, then find the loop and put it over the forward cleat.

• Remember that the rope should go over the boat's

roller, if you have one, to prevent it from chafing over time.

Returning to a Dock
You'll nearly always have less room to maneuver when you come back into a dock, because of the way they're configured and the presence of other boats and other water users; remember that there are likely to be dinghies bobbing out, and boats lining up for fuel and other services.

• The perfect opportunity for approaching a dock will be if you can sidle along parallel with it, into the wind, which will help you to control your stop more effectively.

• You should have your fenders deployed before you start your approach, perhaps giving one of your

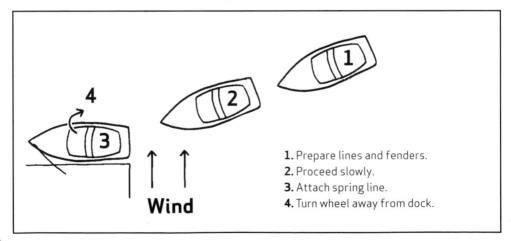

1. Prepare lines and fenders.
2. Proceed slowly.
3. Attach spring line.
4. Turn wheel away from dock.

Wind

Returning to a Beach

There are lots of potential problems here. The changing tide may have shifted the physical composition of the beach so it's harder to haul the boat out, or the water may have become too deep to stand in comfortably, or the wind and waves may both be pushing you hard into shore so you're going too fast. It's usually best to start slowing down (perhaps by dropping sails) earlier than you might think. Keep an eye on the water depth so that you can get your rudder higher in the water and partly pull up the centerboard (if you have one) before they scrape along the bottom. You still need them in the water to help you control the boat; when you come to a stop you can lift them out completely, and then the crew can jump in to steady and then secure the boat while someone fetches the trailer.

crew a spare that can be used as necessary.

• If you're on your own, try and get a friendly passerby to help out (they usually will, because it's good sailing etiquette); otherwise you'll need to step off the boat when it's going slowly enough and start tying up.

• If you can't get a long, smooth, against-the-wind approach, then there are various ways of tying up that can help.

• The person on the dock should never try to slow or stop the boat by themselves, but always tie the line round a secure object to get more leverage.

• If you're forced to use the windward side of the dock, try and get upwind and hope the wind will gently nudge you into position on the dock.

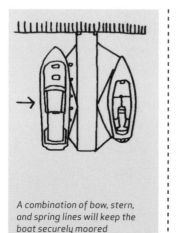

A combination of bow, stern, and spring lines will keep the boat securely moored

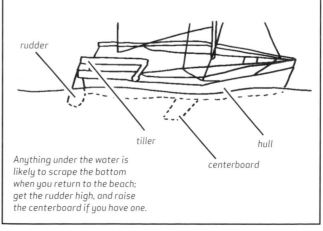

Anything under the water is likely to scrape the bottom when you return to the beach; get the rudder high, and raise the centerboard if you have one.

rudder

tiller

centerboard

hull

SECTION FIVE

Cooking and Provisions

Cooking on Board

Cooking on a boat is a unique experience, and certainly isn't like cooking anywhere else—unless you've tried to cook in the galley of a recreational vehicle while it was moving. (Here's a tip: don't.) Everything is ranged against you: the tiny space, the tinier stove, the movement of the boat, the lack of dish-washing facilities, the heat generated in such a small space, the inherent perils of cooking with dangerous and potentially unstable fuel....

More Safety Tips
- Never leave the stove switched on and unattended. Boats move, and so do pots and pans—even if they're fancy ones designed for use at sea. Most stoves operate at a lower pressure than your one at home, and burners are more easily blown out by the wind.
- Place dampened dish towels under plates to stop them sliding about.
- When you're cooking, you'll need to wedge yourself in somewhere or wear what's called a galley strap so you don't end up falling over!

Meals matter when you're on board. All that fresh air and exercise, the chores, the occasional bouts of boredom—sometimes it feels as though there's not much else to look forward to after a hectic day, so it's important to make them count. Before we get on to the specifics, here are a few simple guidelines we've picked up:

- Eat out when you can—seriously. Boating's supposed to be fun, and it won't be if at the end of every day one of you (it may start out that way, but it usually ends up being the same person, doesn't it, Mom?) ends up sweating away in the galley. Depending on where you are, and the culinary circles you're accustomed to frequent, you may be surprised at how inexpensive a good meal is. And it's a great chance to sample the local cuisine.
- You only need one "proper" sit-down meal in a day. Breakfast can be a nourishing cereal like muesli that will fill you up and is easy to store and prepare; ditto porridge/oatmeal. If you're not eating out, then grab lunch as you go, and make the evening meal the time you sit down together and have dinner.
- Don't overstock. If you're off on a short hop between islands, or a day trip round the headland and along the coast, prepare the food beforehand so it's ready to eat or just needs reheating; even dried camping meals have their place on a boat.
- Don't overstock, part II. You'll end up throwing stuff away, or discovering something disgusting lurking at the back of one of the cupboards a year

past its use-by date. As you go, you'll discover the few things that you can't live without and are hard to get elsewhere; so take them with you.

- Plan a weekly menu (with our help) and rotate it. On pages 76–87 you'll find lots of handy recipes—many of them one-pot ones (or at most two) to help you save space on the stove, and save time and water when you have to wash the dishes.
- Accept that there are some things it'll be harder to get fresh. Use canned meat and fish, but fresh fruit and veg; they're usually easier to get and much easier to store.
- Take a fishing rod and learn how to use it. It's lots of fun, and will help supplement your diet.
- Share the cook's hat around and make whoever does the cooking do the washing up as well. My daughter says

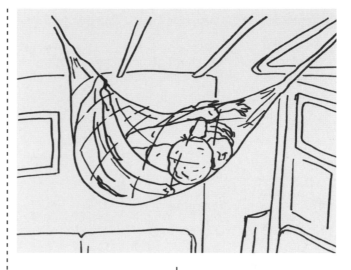

this is "harsh" (well, she says everything's harsh, actually) but it means that whoever's not on duty that day gets a complete break from galley chores. This makes it much more restful.

- Up the portion sizes— people eat more at sea than they do on dry land.

- First time out, consider using paper plates and plastic cutlery to cut down on doing the dishes.
- Wear a plastic apron when you're cooking, a few splashes and spills are far more likely in this relatively unstable environment than in your kitchen at home.

Storage Tips
- Use as few glass containers as you can—they break easily, and the clinking will drive you insane.
- Use see-through, square containers. They make better use of the available space than round ones, and you don't have to open them to see what's inside.
- Anything that attracts moisture, and can go soggy, should be put inside a container inside another container.
- Screw the lids of spice jars to the bottoms of shelves, then screw the jars themselves on and off the lids when you need them.
- Fruit and veg can hang in mesh bags; wrap citrus fruits in foil to keep them fresher for longer; don't mix apples and bananas together because there's a gas in apples that will make the bananas ripen too quickly; don't mix potatoes and onions because the onions cause the spuds to rot.

The Galley: Kitchen Ingredients

Unless you've reached the luxury cruiser class, space is usually the issue here—space and time. Although cooking on board is fun and rewarding, there are usually other things that you'd rather be doing with your time—like swimming or fishing, sunbathing, or bird-watching, or just hanging out, relaxing, and enjoying yourself. So we've tried to choose the following meals carefully so that they combine the maximum amount of taste with the minimum amount of time and effort. That doesn't mean you can't spend all day in the galley. After all, if that's what floats your boat...

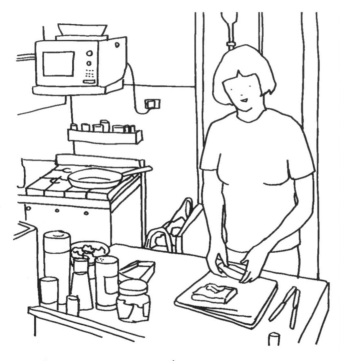

your taste, just as not every recipe will be appropriate for your boat or your trip. What we've tried to do is give a flavor of the kinds of simple but delicious meals—and treats—that work well on board, whether you're on an ocean-going yacht, a funky canal boat, a family river cruiser, or a kayak, pulled to the shore of a quiet lake somewhere.

Pantry List
- oat bran, wheat germ, oatmeal
- croissants, various breads (rolls, French bread, whole-grain, pitas), tortillas
- butter or margarine, powdered milk, yogurt, cream cheese (hard cheese like Parmesan is also good), blue cheese, aged Cheddar, eggs
- good-quality cooking oil
- honey, crunchy peanut butter, jam, pudding, whipped cream
- onions, parsnips, potatoes, asparagus, tomatoes, mushrooms, garlic, tofu, carrots, celery, cucumber, scallions, mint leaves, leaf spinach
- banana, strawberries, walnut halves, kiwi fruit

Fresh Food
Appealing though it may be, fresh food doesn't keep well unless you've got a fridge, and that weighs a ton. The secret here is to use it whenever you can get it and use it straight away. So, if you can catch fish or crabs, or buy fresh from a local market, then make sure you do, and enjoy it that day or the next. Your cooler will do a fair job of keeping food fresh, but you'd do best to think of it as an unplanned treat and use it as soon as you can. Of course, some types of fresh food keep better for longer. We've tried to choose some of those in our list.

Here are the ingredients you'll need in order to make the meals in the recipe section that follows. Not everything here will be to

SECTION FIVE

- salt, pepper, dried mixed herbs, bay leaves, nutmeg, cinnamon, cumin, a steak sauce (such as Worcestershire sauce), pesto, Tabasco®, chocolate bars, sugar (cubes, because loose sugar goes everywhere), lemon juice, balsamic vinegar, curry powder, flour, cornstarch, breadcrumbs, chicken and vegetable bouillon cubes, mustard (Dijon is great), dried chiles, tomato paste
- instant mashed potatoes, dried onions, dried apricots, olives, pancake mix, medium-grained rice, easy-cook noodles, spaghetti, tagliatelle (or your favorite pasta), couscous
- cans of beans (mixed or kidney), chickpeas, sun-dried tomatoes, canned tuna, canned chopped tomatoes, cans of lentils, potatoes, and carrots, canned curry sauces, canned red plums
- ham, sausages, hotdogs, smoked salmon, bacon, chicken pieces, minced and diced pork, fresh fish (when you can buy or catch it), corned beef
- red and white wine (boxes are the most convenient), cider.

Day Trips

If you're out for the afternoon or the day, then food's not really an issue. You can take a few sandwiches or an entire picnic, just as if you were going out to the park, or pack a disposable barbecue and eat in comfort on the lake shore. Although many canal boats have fabulous kitchens—and we mean fabulous—their owners often see an evening meal at a cozy waterside inn as being one of the highlights of the day, and certainly a just reward for negotiating all those locks. And if you're out for a few hours in rough water piloting a little sailing dinghy on your own, then you probably won't have time for anything more than a power bar, anyway!

Dried or Canned?

It depends on how much space you've got, whether weight is an issue, and how easy it's going to be to recycle all those empty cans. Dried foods take up less space but need more preparation, and it's not always convenient to leave a load of chickpeas soaking in a pan of water. Cans are more convenient when it comes to cooking, and their ingredients—as used in these recipes—are tasty enough. The choice is yours, but we usually recommend a mixture of the two.

The Herb Garden

There are now plenty of herbs you can buy as seeds in their own little foil sachets, complete with rich soil and plant food. In this way you can actually have a little herb garden on board and enjoy fresh herbs with your dinner whenever you like: mint, parsley, and basil are all good choices.

Easy Breakfasts

OK, we've established that everyone eats more on a boat. It's the fresh air, it's the exercise—even if you're the one sitting down and the most strenuous thing you do all day is hold a fishing rod—it's the getting away from being landlocked and dragged down. So just enjoy it—especially breakfast, which is designed to give you the fuel to kick-start another day afloat.

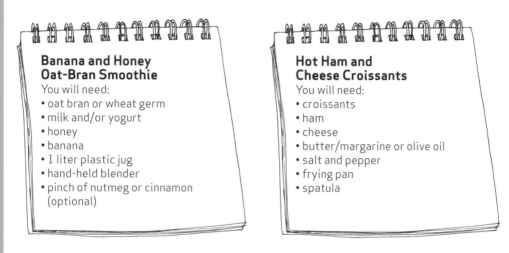

Banana and Honey Oat-Bran Smoothie

You will need:
- oat bran or wheat germ
- milk and/or yogurt
- honey
- banana
- 1 liter plastic jug
- hand-held blender
- pinch of nutmeg or cinnamon (optional)

Hot Ham and Cheese Croissants

You will need:
- croissants
- ham
- cheese
- butter/margarine or olive oil
- salt and pepper
- frying pan
- spatula

No worries if you haven't got a blender—just put all the ingredients (using yogurt instead of milk) into a bowl, and it's still delicious. A fruit smoothie is great for kids because they love to design their own variations, so it's a good way of getting them to eat fruit; in  addition, you can let them get as exotic as they like, since you won't have to eat any of it. Allow one banana per person, cut into small pieces and placed in the jug. Add one mug of milk per person, or some yogurt if preferred, a teaspoon of honey per person, one small spoon of oat bran or wheat germ per person, and a pinch of cinnamon or nutmeg. Blend the ingredients together in the jug, using your hand-held blender, until smooth; then serve.

This recipe is a variation of a toasted sandwich, and which is fried instead of toasted. You only need to use a small amount of butter/margarine or oil—about the same amount as you would if you were making a sandwich. Cut the croissants in half, and butter or oil the outside of the croissant. Fill the middle of the croissant with a slice of ham and a couple of slices of cheese. Lightly oil the frying pan; try covering the end of the oil bottle with a paper towel and quickly tipping the bottle, then wiping the oil onto the pan with the towel. Carefully place the filled croissant into the pan and fry each side on a low heat until it is lightly browned and the cheese has started to melt.

Caution: that filling is hot.

Potato, Egg, and Cheese Bubble and Squeak

You will need:
- box of instant mashed potatoes, or a few leftover spuds
- eggs
- oil
- milk
- water
- cheese, grated
- salt and pepper
- dash of Worcestershire or other hot sauce (optional)
- mixing bowl
- frying pan
- spatula
- wooden spoon
- cheese grater

Fried Bread with Tomatoes, Olives, and Pesto Sauce

You will need:
- French bread
- fresh tomatoes
- pesto
- olive oil
- olives (green or black)
- salt and pepper
- spatula
- mixing bowl
- plate
- frying pan

This is a variation on a traditional British dish, usually made from leftover potato and cabbage. Make up the instant mash in a mixing bowl according to the instructions on the box; or peel and boil potatoes and, when cooked so that a fork goes in easily, mash them in the mixing bowl. Add a cup of grated cheese, two or three eggs, a pinch of salt and pepper, a dash or two of sauce, then mix the whole lot together with a wooden spoon. Heat a dollop of oil in the pan (so that the bottom of the pan is covered in oil, but not swimming in it), then add the mixture. You may have to flatten the mixture out with the wooden spoon to get it to cook evenly. Fry on a low heat, turning the mixture every few minutes to avoid burning, and cook until the eggs have set. You could serve this with baked beans or canned tomatoes.

Not your average choice for breakfast, this Mediterranean-style combination is a healthy alternative that will certainly wake up your taste buds. One advantage of this recipe is that the tomatoes and the pesto mixture can be made the night before, placed in an airtight container, and kept in a fridge or cooler until needed. Slice the tomatoes thinly and place on the plate. Sprinkle tomatoes with salt and pepper to taste. Put a couple of teaspoonfuls of pesto and a dribble of olive oil into a small mixing bowl; this mixture needs to be fairly runny. Slice the required amount of French bread and oil both sides. Gently heat a lightly oiled frying pan, put in the bread, and fry on both sides until golden-brown. Remove the bread from the pan and top with the tomatoes, remembering to add an olive. Finally, dribble the pesto mixture over the top.

Easy Breakfasts continued

Chocolate and Apricot Oatmeal

You will need:
- oatmeal or porridge oats
- milk
- chocolate bars
- dried apricots
- sugar or honey
- saucepan
- wooden spoon
- grater
- small bowl

Cream Cheese and Smoked Salmon Pancakes

You will need:
- box of pancake mix
- smoked salmon
- cream cheese
- lemon juice
- butter/margarine or oil
- mixing bowl
- frying pan
- spatula

The kids will love this, and it will give them a nutritious start to the day. Grate or chop the chocolate (about four squares per person) and place in the small bowl. Then add an extra square to make up for the one that you ate. Chop the apricots into small pieces and add them (allow one or two apricots per person) then add sugar or honey to taste. Measure out a mugful of oats per person (less for kids) and place in the pan over a medium heat. Add the milk, bring to a simmer, and keep stirring with the wooden spoon until the mixture thickens; then continue cooking for a further minute or so. Add the chocolate and apricots, then remove from heat and continue stirring until chocolate has melted.

Prepare the pancake mixture in the small mixing bowl according to the instructions on the box. Heat a very small amount of oil in the frying pan—just enough to wet the bottom of the pan—then add enough pancake mixture to cover the pan and fry until the underneath is brown and set. Flip the pancake over with the spatula and cook the other side until also  brown and set. Transfer the pancake onto the plate and spread with cream cheese, adding a couple of slices of smoked salmon. Roll up the pancake and splash with lemon juice.

Toast Soldiers?

Something that you might like to try, although many Americans consider this to be extremely strange, is the British tradition of boiled eggs with "soldiers" (fingers of buttered toast), which are then dipped into the yolk of the egg. But how come bread that's been toasted, buttered, and then cut into strips is called "soldiers?" Nobody really knows. Although widely used throughout England since the 1950s, the term didn't appear in dictionaries until the mid-1960s. It's possible that lining them up in little rows resembled soldiers on parade, though others have speculated a link with the nursery rhyme "Humpty Dumpty." It remains a popular part of a traditional British breakfast.

Boiled Eggs with Asparagus Dippers
You will need:
• eggs
• asparagus
• butter
• medium-sized saucepan
• water
• wooden spoon
• shallow dish or plate
• egg cups

One-Pan Sailors' Breakfast
You will need:
• eggs
• bacon
• sausages
• mushrooms
• olive oil
• mixing bowl
• frying pan
• spatula
• wooden spoon

This is a very simple and delicious variation on a favorite traditional English breakfast. Best of all, the fact that it only uses one pan means that there is less work for whoever is cleaning the dishes! Half-fill the pan with water and bring to a boil. In the meantime, prepare the asparagus by cutting off the tough stems, then carefully place them into the pan of water and boil for between two and four minutes. When the asparagus is crisp–tender, carefully remove from the boiling water, place on the plate, and spread with butter; leave to cool. In the meantime, carefully place the eggs into the water and boil for three or four minutes. Place into egg cups, gently crack and remove the top of the egg, and dip the asparagus into the egg as you would bread sticks.

Cut the bacon, sausages, and mushrooms into small pieces. Beat a couple of eggs—one per person—in the mixing bowl. Place a dollop of oil into the frying pan and heat slowly. Add the bacon and sausages and fry gently, turning occasionally with the spatula until almost cooked. This will take about five to seven minutes. Then add the mushrooms and continue cooking for a couple more minutes until the mushrooms are cooked. Add the beaten eggs to the pan and stir around a bit so that the egg mixture reaches the bottom of the pan. When the eggs have set, it's ready. Serve with crusty bread, pitas, or tortillas.

Drinking Water
You should drink plenty of water when you're on board, and, despite various attempts to come up with an alternative solution, that means water in plastic bottles. You should drink little and often—the theory being that you ration thirst, not water. In other words, don't wait till you're thirsty before you take a drink. An adult needs upward of four pints (two liters) of water a day, although exactly how much clearly depends on your sex, physique, level of activity, the weather conditions and so on.

SECTION FIVE

Quick Lunches

The emphasis here is on speed, because people are often so busy having fun that they don't think they can make time to do any "real" cooking. Hopefully the recipes on the following pages will serve as a reminder that it's the love and the thought that makes a meal great—and not the time you spend slaving over it.

Chicken (or Tofu) Noodle Soup
You will need:
• one or two chicken breasts, or tofu
• one onion
• one large carrot
• one stick of celery
• a block of noodles, or a small fistful of spaghetti broken into short lengths
• a chicken or vegetable bouillon cube
• water
• oil
• pepper
• saucepan
• wooden spoon

Couscous Salad with Minted Yogurt
You will need:
• small packet of couscous
• pan of boiling water
• one small cucumber
• four small tomatoes
• one bunch of scallions or one small onion
• lemon juice
• splash of olive oil
• one carton of plain Greek yogurt
• fresh mint leaves
• heatproof serving dish
• wooden spoon and fork
• salt and pepper

You can adapt this recipe to taste: add any variety of vegetable, and replace the chicken with tofu for the vegetarians. Peel and chop the carrot into matchstick pieces, peel and finely chop the onion, and thinly slice the celery. Then slice the chicken into thin strips. Heat a dollop of oil in the saucepan and add all the prepared ingredients, except the noodles. Gently fry for a couple of minutes, until the chicken has browned, stirring continuously. Add water to nearly fill the pan and crumble the bouillon cube into it. Simmer for about ten minutes, then add the noodles or spaghetti, cook for a further five minutes, or until the pasta is done, and serve.

This is great because it requires barely any cooking. You can also adapt this recipe by omitting the yogurt and mint and making up a salad dressing of your own choice instead.

Finely chop the cucumber, tomatoes, scallions or onion, and mint. Mix the chopped mint and lemon juice in with the yogurt. Place the couscous into a heatproof serving dish, pour in boiling water—enough to cover the couscous—and let it stand for five minutes. Fluff up the grains with the fork, then add the chopped cucumber, tomatoes, and onion. Then add the yogurt mix and carefully mix together. It's lovely served with pita bread, or you can fry up a couple of lamb chops or lamb sausages to go with it.

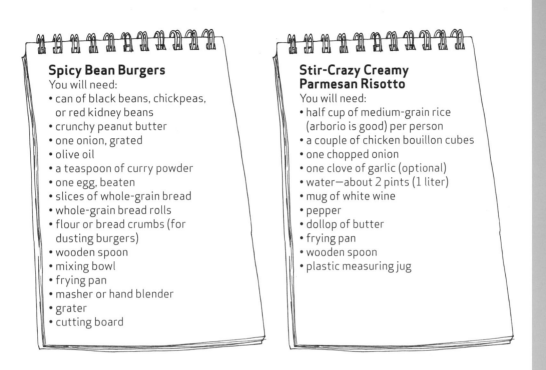

Spicy Bean Burgers

You will need:

- can of black beans, chickpeas, or red kidney beans
- crunchy peanut butter
- one onion, grated
- olive oil
- a teaspoon of curry powder
- one egg, beaten
- slices of whole-grain bread
- whole-grain bread rolls
- flour or bread crumbs (for dusting burgers)
- wooden spoon
- mixing bowl
- frying pan
- masher or hand blender
- grater
- cutting board

Stir-Crazy Creamy Parmesan Risotto

You will need:

- half cup of medium-grain rice (arborio is good) per person
- a couple of chicken bouillon cubes
- one chopped onion
- one clove of garlic (optional)
- water—about 2 pints (1 liter)
- mug of white wine
- pepper
- dollop of butter
- frying pan
- wooden spoon
- plastic measuring jug

Open the can of beans and drain the juice from the can, then empty the beans into  the mixing bowl along with a couple of dollops of peanut butter and the curry powder. Tear the bread up into small pieces and add it to the mixing bowl along with the egg. Mash this mixture together as best you can; you may have to get your hands messy here, so make sure they're clean. It's easier to mix with your hands once you've mashed the bean mix. You can use a hand blender if you have one. Peel and grate the onion and mix it in with the rest of the mixture using a wooden spoon. Sprinkle some flour onto a cutting board, and with floured hands shape about four to six burgers. Pour enough oil to cover the bottom of the frying pan, and heat slowly. Add the burgers and cook on a medium heat for about five to seven minutes, turning once halfway through. Serve the burgers in buns, adding mayonnaise, lettuce, tomato, and mustard.

This recipe can be easily adapted—for example, adding a few juicy prawns. All you need to remember here is to keep stirring, add the liquid slowly, and you can't go wrong.

Boil enough water to dissolve the stock cubes, and put both water and cubes into the plastic jug. Peel, thinly slice, and chop the onion and garlic (if you're using it). On the lowest heat, put a large dollop of butter into the pan and let it melt. Add the onions and garlic and gently fry, stirring continuously with a wooden spoon, until the onions are soft—it's important not to let the butter burn. Remove the pan from the heat, measure out the rice, and add it to the pan. Return to a low heat and allow the rice to cook for a couple of minutes. Again, continue to stir and don't let it burn. Add the bouillon and the mug of wine slowly, and stir. Continue to add water slowly until rice has absorbed it and is soft. Remove from the heat, stir in the grated cheese, add a sprinkle of pepper, and serve.

Quick Lunches continued

Fishcakes
You will need:
• can of tuna
• box of instant mashed potatoes
• one egg, beaten
• oil
• salt and pepper
• one cup of cornstarch
• wooden spoon
• spatula
• frying pan
• salt and pepper
• mixing bowl
• cutting board

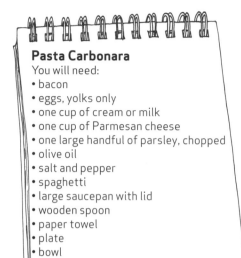

Pasta Carbonara
You will need:
• bacon
• eggs, yolks only
• one cup of cream or milk
• one cup of Parmesan cheese
• one large handful of parsley, chopped
• olive oil
• salt and pepper
• spaghetti
• large saucepan with lid
• wooden spoon
• paper towel
• plate
• bowl

In the mixing bowl, make up the mashed potatoes according to the instructions on the box. Add to the bowl the tuna, egg, half a cup of cornstarch, a pinch of salt and pepper, and mix the ingredients together with the wooden spoon. Use the remaining cornstarch to dust the cutting board and your hands, then shape about four to six fishcakes. If you find the mixture a bit gooey, then add a little bit more flour. Put enough oil in the pan to cover the bottom, and place on a low heat. Carefully place the fishcakes in the pan and fry for about five minutes on each side. You can serve these in a bread roll or pita bread, with baked beans or a simple green salad.

In a bowl, beat the egg yolks and cream or milk together, then add a pinch of black pepper and set aside. Chop the bacon up into small pieces. Drizzle a small amount of oil into the bottom of the large saucepan and place on a low heat. When the oil's hot, add the bacon and fry on a medium heat until crispy. Remove the bacon and drain on a plate covered with paper towel. With another piece of paper towel, wipe out the bottom of the pan to remove any remaining oil. Half-fill the pan with water, add a pinch of salt, and bring to a boil. When the water is boiling, add the spaghetti and cook for the time recommended on the packet. If you haven't got a colander, drain the spaghetti using the saucepan lid to keeping the pasta from slipping out. Immediately add the beaten yolk mixture to the spaghetti and return to the heat. Stir over a medium heat for about a minute, then add the Parmesan cheese and chopped parsley. Stir again and serve.

Delicious Evening Meals

These are a little more elaborate, but with a little preparation they need be barely any more arduous than the quick lunches on the previous pages. Remember those healthy boating appetites—especially on the fools who skipped lunch—and then take a look at the people on the boat. If you think they need feeding up, increase the portion sizes accordingly.

Chicken with Olive, Tomato, and Basil (serves 4)
You will need:
• four chicken breasts
• a can of chopped tomatoes
• about 20 green or black olives
• one clove of garlic
• olive oil
• one cup of red or white wine
• salt and pepper
• a few leaves of fresh basil or half a teaspoonful of dried mixed herbs
• a large, deep non-stick frying pan with lid
• spatula
• paper towel

Quick Lamb Curry (serves 4)
You will need:
• jar of korma, rogan josh, or madras curry sauce (depending on whether you like it mild, medium, or hot)
• one package of stewing lamb
• an onion
• oil
• one small carton of plain yogurt
• a packet of boil-in-the-bag rice, or a can of rice
• large frying pan with lid
• saucepan
• wooden spoon

This is a very quick and easy dish to prepare. Peel and roughly chop the garlic, then chop the basil leaves and set aside. Pour some oil onto some kitchen roll and wipe the bottom of the pan with it. Gently heat the pan, then add the chicken pieces and fry on a medium heat for about 5 minutes, turning once during cooking. Open the can of tomatoes and add to the pan along with the garlic, basil or dried herbs, olives, and wine. Add a pinch of salt and pepper and stir with the wooden spoon, then cover with the pan lid. Reduce the heat to low and simmer for about ten minutes. Serve this with salad, potatoes, or spaghetti.

You can make quick and simple curries using ready-prepared sauces and meat or vegetables of your own choice. If you use cubed meat, the curry will be cooked in half the time. Here's one to get you started.

Pour a small amount of oil into the frying pan, chop the onions, then fry them until soft. Add the lamb to the pan and fry until it has browned. Open the jar of curry sauce and pour over the meat, then stir, put the lid on the pan, and simmer for about 20 minutes. Stir occasionally, so that the meat doesn't stick to the bottom of the pan. In the meantime, either open the can of rice and heat slowly, or place the boil-in-the-bag rice into a pan of boiling water and boil for about six minutes. Just before you serve, stir in the plain yogurt to the curry. Serve this with pita bread.

Delicious Evening Meals continued

Pan-Fried Fillet of Fish with Lemon Butter Sauce
You will need:
- one fish fillet per person
- butter
- lemon juice
- flour for dusting fish
- salt and pepper
- parsley (optional)
- spatula
- teaspoon
- wooden spoon
- cutting board
- paper towel

Pork with Plum and Cider Stew
You will need:
- 1 lb lean pork
- one large onion
- two large carrots
- two large parsnips
- one large potato
- one bay leaf
- one can of red plums
- one can of dry cider
- one teaspoon of Dijon mustard
- half a cup of cornstarch
- olive oil
- large frying pan with lid
- wooden spoon

Lightly sprinkle the fish with flour, salt, and pepper, then rub in a few pieces of soft butter. Heat a small amount of oil in the pan, then carefully add the fish, buttered side down. Cook on a medium heat for about one or two minutes, then turn the fish and continue to fry for a further one or two minutes. Remove the pan from the heat and place the fish on a plate. Pour off any oil left in the pan. Add one piece of butter for each piece of fish, and cook over a low heat until the butter is a nutty brown color; then add some lemon juice and chopped parsley before pouring the mixture over your fish. Serve with a salad and boiled potatoes.

Open the can of plums and remove the pits, then cut in half and set to one side. Peel all the vegetables and chop into fairly small cubes, then set aside. Chop the pork into small cubes and also set aside. Pour enough oil to cover the bottom of the pan. Heat the oil over a medium heat and fry the pork cubes until just browned. Add the chopped onion and fry for about two minutes. Add all the other chopped vegetables and fry for a further five minutes. Stir, and then add the plums, cider, and bay leaf to the pan. Leave to simmer in the pot on a medium heat for about 40 minutes. Before serving, add the cornstarch and Dijon mustard, then stir until the sauce has thickened.

Speedy Stir-Fries
Many food stores offer a range of ready-prepared stir-fry vegetables and sauces. Just add some peeled shrimp or strips of chicken, and away you go. The method of cooking is simple: all you need is a frying pan and a small amount of oil—sesame or peanut oil is best.

Heat the oil in a pan. If you're using prawns or meat, fry these for a few minutes, then add the vegetables and cook for a further couple of minutes, stirring continuously, until they just start to soften. Add the sauce right at the end, and serve with rice or noodles.

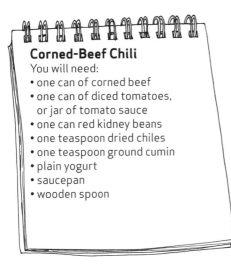

Corned-Beef Chili
You will need:
- one can of corned beef
- one can of diced tomatoes, or jar of tomato sauce
- one can red kidney beans
- one teaspoon dried chiles
- one teaspoon ground cumin
- plain yogurt
- saucepan
- wooden spoon

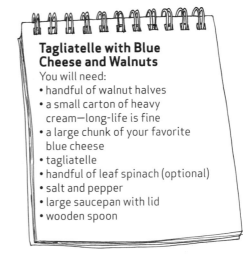

Tagliatelle with Blue Cheese and Walnuts
You will need:
- handful of walnut halves
- a small carton of heavy cream—long-life is fine
- a large chunk of your favorite blue cheese
- tagliatelle
- handful of leaf spinach (optional)
- salt and pepper
- large saucepan with lid
- wooden spoon

This recipe is ready in a flash and couldn't be easier. If you're a vegetarian, just use the kidney beans instead of the beef. Open the can of corned beef, the can of tomatoes, and the can of kidney beans (ah, the Cordon-Bleu-ness of it all!), then empty the can of tomatoes into the saucepan. Roughly chop up the corned beef, then add that to the saucepan also. Place the pan on a low heat and stir until the corned beef has completely broken up; then add the chillies, cumin powder, and beans. Stir on a medium heat for about five to seven minutes. Just before serving, pour in the plain yogurt to taste. Serve with either a can of rice or boil-in-the-bag rice, or in bowls with pita bread.

This recipe is very easy and quick to make. Set a large saucepan half-full of water on the stove and heat until boiling, then add a pinch of salt along with the tagliatelle. While the water is heating, gather together the walnuts, cream, cheese, and spinach if you have some. Break up the cheese into crumbles and set aside. When the tagliatelle is cooked according to the instructions on the packet, remove from the heat and drain, using the lid of the pan to stop the tagliatelle from sliding out. Add the cream, cheese, walnuts, and leaf spinach to the pan. Return to the lowest heat and mix together so that all the tagliatelle is covered, then add a pinch or two of pepper and serve.

Barbecue!
Barbecued food is amazing after a long, enjoyable day on the water, and it's also one of the healthiest ways to cook all kinds of meat and vegetables. It requires almost no culinary skill to make good hamburgers or veggie kebabs, and it's a good opportunity for everyone to get involved in the food preparation and the actual cooking. And at the end, there's a lot less to clean up!

Treats Afloat

These are just the job when people are worn out, or just sleepy, or maybe need a little pick-me-up. They're good for helping kids get to sleep after a long day, or as a reward for a late-night session on watch. Just make sure that there's some serious teeth-brushing before anyone goes to sleep.

Fruit Dipped in Melted Chocolate

Peel and chop any fruit you like, and set aside. Then you can melt the chocolate in one of two ways: (1) Break up the chocolate and place in a heatproof bowl, which you then set over a pan of boiling water. Let the chocolate melt in the bowl, then carefully remove the bowl from the heat. (2) Break up the chocolate into small pieces and place in a small pan, melt the chocolate over a very low heat, then remove from the heat. Then with a fork take a piece of fruit and dip into the melted chocolate—yummy.

Pound Cake with Crème Fraiche and Kiwi Fruit

This one will stop you getting scurvy (OK, only joking), as kiwi fruit are rich in vitamin C.

Peel and slice a couple of kiwi fruit and set to one side. Slice a store-bought pound cake longways and then, if you're lucky enough to have a bottle of sweet wine, sherry, or even a drop of brandy on board, sprinkle a few drops onto each half of the cake. Spread some crème fraiche on each of the halves of cake, then put slices of kiwi fruit on top of that. Put the two slices of cake back together and slice into portions. Steady on!

The Beauty of Cookies

The great joy of cookies is that they're so versatile and can be transformed into many favorite desserts. That's always assuming you can keep the crew away from them in their "raw" form. Here are a few ideas:

• Cookie Banoffee

This will keep the kids happy (the big ones too), and they will love making them, so long as you do the difficult stuff at home first. Before you leave land, boil up several unopened cans of sweetened condensed milk in a large pan. You need to boil for at least two hours (it's worth it, believe me), and make sure you keep topping the pan up with boiling water so it doesn't boil dry. Condensed milk prepared in this way will keep indefinitely, so it's worth preparing a couple of cans. Then when you need one, open the can and you'll find a delicious golden-brown gooey toffee. Slice some pieces of banana, place on a cookie, and top with a spoonful of toffee; you can also add a squirt of whipped cream if you wish.

• Lemon-Curd Shortbreads

Take a packet of shortbread cookies, spread them with lemon curd, and top with whipped cream.

• Amaretti Biscuits with Poached Peach Halves

A good one to make when you've just had a fight with the nearest and dearest! Take a packet of amaretti biscuits (any kind of cookies will do, but these almond ones are particularly tasty) and smash to pieces. You can do this by putting them into a plastic bag and hitting them with a rolling pin. Put the smashed cookies into a bowl and add a teaspoon or two of honey, then mix together and put to one side. Open a can of peach halves and pour into a pan, adding a drop of brandy or a slug of wine. Heat the peaches slowly for a couple of minutes. Remove from heat, place in a bowl, and carefully add the cookie mixture to the centre of each peach half. This is even more delicious if you top with a dollop of crème fraiche.

Easy Rice Pudding

Melt a dollop of butter into a large pan, stir in some arborio rice, and cook on a low heat for a couple of minutes. Add enough milk to cover the rice, and continue to stir until the milk has been absorbed into the rice. Continue to cook the rice like this, adding milk as you go, until the rice is tender and creamy. It usually takes about 30 minutes. Once cooked, you can add a variety of goodies, such as: flakes of chocolate, squirts of cream, fruit of your choice, and not forgetting that good old favorite, strawberry jam.

Pineapple in Toffee Sauce

Open a can of pineapple rings and pour the juice off into a pan. Add a cup of water to this and about three cups of brown sugar, stir, and bring to the boil. Continue stirring, and when the sugar has dissolved add a teaspoonful of vinegar and a large chunk of butter. Continue to boil for a few more minutes and remove from the heat. Pour the mixture over the pineapple and serve. Be careful, it'll be hot!

Sponge Cake with Hot Lemon Sauce

You can use any pre-made sponge cake for this. Mix together the juice of two lemons with one tablespoonful of cornstarch and one of sugar; you can, if you wish, add some lemon zest by finely grating it. Melt a stick of butter in a pan on a low heat, then pour in the lemon and cornstarch mixture. Keep stirring until it thickens. If it gets too thick, just add more juice or a little water. Pour over the sliced cake and serve.

Hot Chocolate with Marshmallow and More Chocolate

This really is an old-time favorite with a twist—once you've had it, you'll wonder why you don't have it more often. Still, if you've been hard at it all day, or maybe just started a long watch, you can treat yourself and forget your waistband for once. Make the hot chocolate according to the instructions on the can or packet, then add some mini marshmallows, or cut up a couple of big ones and drop the pieces into the chocolate. Then—and here's the good bit—drop in a few pieces of milk chocolate or any other favorite chocolate bar. Now you could finish it off with a good blast of canned cream, but that might be an indulgence too far. If you have an audience, you may use a spoon; otherwise, dive in.

Dutch-Oven Cookery

If you're planning on combining a boating trip with some camping, why not take a Dutch oven with you? When it comes to campfire cooking, this is the most valuable, most versatile cooking pot you'll find. The average Dutch oven has a handle which can hang from a rod over the fire, and stubby legs which allow it to sit right over hot coals. You can make just about anything in a Dutch oven, and this one-pot style of cooking is perfect for a campsite where dish-washing facilities are primitive. Line it with oil and layer pork ribs, chicken, and then beef ribs and a good slosh of barbecue sauce; cook steak and potatoes in the same way, or lasagne (yes, really), deep-dish pizzas, or chicken with rice. There's almost nothing that you can't cook in a Dutch oven.

SECTION FIVE

Waste Disposal

Waste on the water is a hot topic. Human beings are great at creating the stuff but generally have a poor track record when it comes to dealing with it responsibly. In many regions there are strict regulations concerning waste disposal, but most boating happens away from the eyes of the regulators and lawmakers and it's up to individual sailors to behave responsibly and do the right thing.

So what is waste? Most marine organizations break it down as follows:

• **Garbage**
Leftover food, empty glass bottles, tins, and other packaging, broken glassware and crockery, cloth of any description.

• **Dishwater**
Assuming you scrape plates and other utensils and cookware before washing, it's the water that's left over; otherwise this is usually called:

• **Grey water**
From the dishwasher, shower, washbasins (but not toilets).

Small portable toilets like this are easy to maintain and easy to empty, making them a good solution for small boats.

• **Plastic**
Any biodegradable or non-degradable plastic, such as polystyrene cups, six-pack holders, milk jugs—even ropes and lines.

• **Dunnage**
Less relevant to most leisure sailors, this is waste associated with cargo.

What Do I Do with My Waste?

Amazingly, if you're more than 25 miles out to sea you can dump almost anything you like in the water apart from plastic, but make sure that you dispose of your waste responsibly for the sake of those who follow you and the environment.

Pack It Out

Hikers and camping enthusiasts have known about this stuff for years, and it's no different if you're spending a few days fishing at a remote lake or drifting down the river in a canoe and sleeping under the stars for a couple of nights. Nature doesn't want your trash, so anything that won't degrade quickly and naturally needs to go home with you or be disposed of properly at the trailhead or park entrance. Dumping the remains of your dinner—or the cans it came in—in the bushes will attract wild animals to your camp and possibly harm them. Burn empty cans in the fire to remove food traces and then stamp them flat, and scatter any leftovers far away from the camp. Dig a hole at least 200 ft away from any fresh water, and pour your dishwater and other waste water into that.

How the Head Works

Your marine sanitation device (MSD), to give it its proper name, must be rigged so that waste cannot be expelled directly into the water. This is crucial, because human waste should never be dumped in inland waters (most territories are still happy to let you dump it so long as you're more than three nautical miles from the shore, however). MSDs come in different types. Portable toilets simply collect the waste in a tank which must later be removed and emptied by hand; Type III toilets are the most common and require the waste to be pumped out at a proper "reception facility;" Type IIs and Type Is treat the waste more efficiently, so that in the latter case it can be discharged overboard. As always with anything important like this, please check your local regulations and comply with them.

For day-to-day waste, all that's necessary is to implement a waste-management plan. This is a very grandiose way of saying that it needs to be someone's responsibility to sort the waste out while you're on board, store it safely, and then dispose of it properly when you return to land. The United States Coast Guard, for example, has a standard waste-management plan where the key paragraph reads: "Waste for this vessel is collected [insert where] and stored [insert location]. When moored, all waste will be carried from the vessel and disposed of [location of dumpster, etc.]. Plastics and waste containing plastic materials will never be discharged into the water from this vessel regardless of location."

Some territories have a more enlightened approach to waste than others, so it may make it easier in the long run if you separate your garbage into stuff to throw away and stuff to be recycled. Then you may be able to separate the recycled stuff into different types such as glass, paper, and cardboard ... that kind of thing. That way, when you get to a recycling point, it'll be easier to put them in their various containers. Other tips include removing all unnecessary packaging before leaving shore, crushing empty cans, taking one large water container and decanting into smaller ones, and turning leftover food into soup instead of throwing it out.

- Waterside Attractions
- Aquatic Scavenger Hunt
- Semaphore Flag Code
- Castaway for a Day
- Supervised Activities
- Fishing

- Watching Wildlife
- Measuring Wind Speed
- Making a Telescope
- Swimming
- Ghost Stories, Sea Shanties, and Games
- Celestial Navigation

SECTION SIX

Activities and Skills

Waterside Attractions

Unless you're in a race or out on the ocean, you probably won't want to spend all day every day in or on your boat. Fortunately there's always plenty to do by the water, and although you may need some extra cash to cover excursions, there are also plenty of things to do that cost nothing—or at least next to nothing. Try this selection of ideas.

Marinas

These are more than just places to moor up, empty out, and pick up fuel and supplies—they're little communities full of people rather like you who enjoy the life afloat and are usually happy to exchange a tale or two and dispense valuable advice when asked. Marina facilities vary, but you may be lucky enough to find a gym or a pool and various associated activities. Anglers, and those pursuing a particular type of water (kayakers, for example), can usually find intelligence at the local bait or boat shop, and there's generally someone around who knows the very thing that you need to know.

Local Attractions

Arriving in a new town by car can be rather stressful, particularly if it's busy, the roads and signs are unfamiliar, and it's hard to park. By contrast, coming in somewhere by boat is usually far more relaxing. Boating people are naturally accommodating when it comes to taking a line or helping you get the lie of the land, and will advise you about any local regulations and then tell you the best places to visit or eat. Coming in by river or sea is often the best way to see the older part of town, and is a great way to get acquainted quickly with many of the more interesting nooks and crannies.

Exotic Attractions

For those traveling further afield, there are few better ways to explore the Mediterranean or Caribbean than from the deck of a boat. You can run to your own timetable rather than someone else's, there's no need to book a hotel, you can change your plans on a dime, stay in one place as long as you like, even change the "shape" of your holiday entirely by resting up for a few days and taking day trips on land. Talk to other sailors to find out the best places to go, hook up with others to share the kids out and get some time to yourselves, or meet like-minded singles and couples and have a ball.

Aquatic Scavenger Hunt

This simple game works on lots of levels. It's straightforward fun for adults—especially competitive ones—and makes good educational sense for kids. You can also tailor it to suit your environment, dialing the level of difficulty up or down as conditions dictate and increasing or decreasing the number of objects in the hunt depending on how much time you've got.

| pine cone | twig | bird's nest | animal track |
| feather | birds | tree leaf | berry |

What is a Scavenger Hunt?

If you've never played before, it's simple. Make a list of things that everyone has to find, and print it out. Assign scores to each item on the list, depending on how difficult you think it's going to be to find—for example, a starfish washed up on the beach might be worth ten points, whereas a length of seaweed would only be worth two. What you put on the list depends very much on where you are, but there are usually plenty of interesting items, no matter what environment you're in.

Decide on your items and then work out how the competitors can prove that they've completed the hunt by finding everything on the list. If it's a simple game, then you can deliberately choose items that people can bring back to the boat—always assuming that they can be removed safely from their habitat; a round stone with a hole in it is fine, an egg from a bird's nest is not. As an alternative, you can get younger kids to draw the items on the list and then have fun—quite possibly at their expense—trying to guess what they are. Adults can take photos of the items they're searching for—using a digital camera with a decent-sized screen, so that the judges can check without needing a computer or a printer to hand. Just make sure you delete all the items from the camera each time, in case the next hunt includes some of them again, and someone is tempted to cheat.

You can pep up the competition for adults by making some of their tasks more difficult—for example, shooting a photograph of an event, such as an animal coming down to the water to drink, or a spider spinning a web—or by setting a useful task, like catching a fish for tea. If you're away on the boat for a few days, or take regular short trips, you can have a league table and award a prize to the person who wins the most points over the course of the "season."

Semaphore Flag Code

Originally invented as a military communications system in France in the late 1700s, semaphore flags eventually found favor with both the navy (they were used at the battle of Trafalgar in 1805) and the armies in the American Civil War. Portable, easy to operate, and usually easy to see, semaphore flags are a fun way to communicate and a good memory skill to have.

You can still buy semaphore flags from some specialized suppliers, but if you're unable to find them you can make your own from white card, some paints, and a few other bits and bobs. Cut out a square of white card and then rule a line from corner to corner across it. Paint one half yellow and the other half red; put it aside to dry. Get a couple of doweling rods and attach the dried flags to these, either with glue or, if you don't have the patience to wait for it to dry, with a staple gun. Your flags are now ready for use.

The full semaphore alphabet is shown below. All of the letters are spelled using both hands, each of which is placed in one of eight set positions. These positions have been designed so that at no point do the two flags overlap one another. The rest position, used as a pause between words, is simply to hold the flags crossed over and pointing downward.

Why did semaphore fall out of favor? On land, the main reason was expense—the semaphore towers needed to be manned all the time, and the people there had to be paid even when there were no messages being sent. In addition, you couldn't see the flags at night or in bad weather. Worst of all— especially for the military— the messages weren't secret, as anyone who knew the alphabet could read what you were saying to each other.

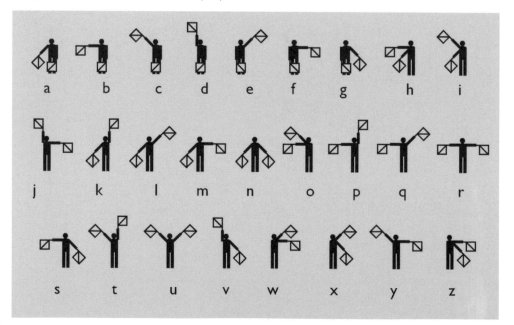

a   b   c   d   e   f   g   h   i

j   k   l   m   n   o   p   q   r

s   t   u   v   w   x   y   z

Castaway for a Day

This is great fun for everyone, it gives adults a break if they need it, it allows the kids some freedom to look after themselves, but it also lets you keep an eye on them. It doesn't have to last an entire day, but can go on longer if the kids are enjoying themselves.

In a perfect world, the idea goes something like this. You wake the kids up and blindfold them. Carefully you lead or carry them down to the dinghy and proceed to shore, where you help them out. You tell them to stand facing in to shore and then wait for your signal. The adults move off from the shore and head back to the main boat. When they're a hundred yards offshore, they shout to the kids to take the blindfolds off. They spin round and find themselves marooned on the beach while you row away. They have become castaways!

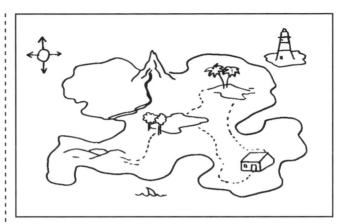

Variations

- Obviously you don't want to upset little kids, so there are various things you can do to reassure them, yet still provide that frisson of excitement. An adult can be a castaway with them and play along with the game; the adults can have their own camp further up the beach; or you can all be marooned together in the same camp.
- Bury their supplies beforehand and give them a treasure map; tell them they have to solve the clues in order to find their camping gear and food.
- Give them a walkie-talkie and use it to communicate the tasks they have to accomplish.
- Older kids are ripe for tricks: when they've bedded down for the night, create a set of footprints that goes right into the camp and out again, for them to discover in the morning when they wake up.
- You can achieve much the same effect by mooring overnight near some woods and letting them camp there, or just spend the afternoon messing about. Even if the weather's warm, you should still make sure they've got a shelter—preferably a tent with insect netting to keep biting insects out.
- Always keep an eye on them, especially if you've decided they can light a fire; make sure everyone's got their own flashlight as well.
- Let really little kids join in the fun by creating a camp for them on the boat.

Things to Do

Looking for things for them to do? They can try and catch a fish for their supper, dress up as pirates and play games, do some face painting—lions, tigers and parrots are good—or you can extend the buried treasure theme and have a visiting adult "accidentally" drop a map on the beach after they've come to check everything's OK. The more the kids think it's not supposed to be part of the game, the more they'll enjoy themselves.

Supervised Activities

At one time, time spent on or near the water was pretty easy to parcel out. You could sunbathe, go swimming (even snorkeling if you lived somewhere nice), or mess about in a boat. Now, thanks to the ingenuity of water lovers, the possibilities are far more wide-ranging. Here's our selection of widely available activities that we think you'll enjoy.

Windsurfing

You'll need to be reasonably fit, but in the hands of a good instructor you should be able to sail, steer, and turn in only a few hours. It's also an excellent way for youngsters to appreciate how sails can work with or against the wind.

Waterskiing

Requires a reasonable level of fitness, but is fantastic fun. You don't need to be a brilliant swimmer, but you do need to be comfortable in the water, as you'll not only get wet, but will be thoroughly dumped, dunked, and sunk more times than you thought was possible. You may come across a fun variation called hydrofoiling which involves a single ski that can be made to leap out of the water, even at speeds as low as 10 mph (16 kph/8.5 knots).

Personal Watercraft

Jet Skis® and other personal watercraft can be wonderful fun, like driving a motorbike. Make sure that you always wear a personal flotation device (PFD)—and goggles, because the spray gets everywhere. In addition, you should always make sure there's a safety lanyard that works; this immediately cuts the power from the engine when you fall off.

Surfing

Surprisingly hard at first, so look for a nice, slowly shelving beach with gentle waves so you can stand up

if you need to. Good schools provide surf shirts and even wetsuits, if conditions require them, as part of the price. Experienced instructors can teach people as young as five and as old as 60, so age is not necessarily an impediment.

Parasailing

Sometimes called parascending, this involves hanging from a parachute while being towed through the air by a fast boat. As with anything to do with flying, the trickiest part is taking off and landing, but thanks to new larger parachutes with lower drag, the towing boat doesn't have to pick up as much speed; in fact, some modern parasail operations allow you to take off and land from the back of the boat, courtesy of a fancy hydraulic system. Parasailing started life as a solo sport, but now most rides take two people or more at a time. The key thing to check here is the quality of the equipment and the qualifications of the boat captain—good schools will have the equivalent of a license from the Coast Guard or similar body.

Tubing

One of the most fun, and least skillful, water-based activities known to humankind, this involves being towed behind a fast boat while sitting or laying in some kind of inflatable (usually a giant rubber-ring-style tube, hence the name) and hanging on for dear life. Because there's very little you can do as a passenger apart from hanging

on, it's very important that the person running the boat knows what they're doing. (Hint: if they're chatting on their cell phone while dragging someone behind, then the answer's probably "No.") In addition, boats should have a spotter to watch the tube and keep an eye on anyone who comes off. All passengers will be wearing a PFD so they should be fine, but there's always the slight chance that someone will get a nasty knock when they come flying out into the water at speed.

Seasoned tubers will often say that it's not a safe activity for kids under six years old, or for slightly built kids even if they are older; and to begin with, boats should keep their speed to under 10 mph (16 kph/8 knots).

Before you join in, spend a little time watching the boat. If the driver is constantly zigzagging or making sharp turns in order to spill passengers deliberately, go and do something else.

Safety First

Naturally there are certain factors to keep in mind:

- Make sure that kids only do the things that are appropriate for their age, height, and physical abilities; in many places, for example, under-18s simply aren't allowed to rent jet skis.
- Try to find out whether the instructors are qualified, or just enthusiastic amateurs rented for the summer (this is easier in some places than others).
- Be aware that in some environments there will be dangers such as submerged coral reefs, jellyfish, strong currents, and powerful surf.
- In theory, it should be the instructor's responsibility to agree to teach only when the conditions are correct, but in some places the culture may encourage a lax attitude, so you should also exercise your own judgment.
- Finally, if it's an activity like parasailing that carries certain risks, check whether the instructors are properly licensed and insured (again, this may be more difficult to ascertain in some places).

Fishing

Although experienced sailors always say you should never rely on fishing as a source of food when you're on a boat, in case the gods of angling don't smile down on you and you go hungry instead, there's no doubt that the thought of fresh fish or seafood will cheer nearly everyone up. But fishing's more than that, particularly if it's not something you do very often—it's a chance for adults and kids to learn a new skill together and have fun while they're doing it. Treat every catch as a bonus, and you won't be disappointed.

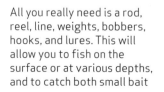

All you really need is a rod, reel, line, weights, bobbers, hooks, and lures. This will allow you to fish on the surface or at various depths, and to catch both small bait and pan fish as well as larger predators. If you're not getting bites, try altering the depth between the bobber and the hook, switch baits, or try somewhere else. If you're fishing with a lure and nothing's happening, change to a different one—some lures are designed to dive, others to splash enticingly along the surface of the

Hand-Lining

You don't have to use a rod and reel, of course. Fishing enthusiasts all over the world have caught plenty on hand lines, which you can buy from tourist shops and then lower over the side of the boat. As an alternative, you can make your own by tying some line around a bottle or can and then wrapping the line around it as if it were a spool. With a decent lead weight on the end, you can strip off a short length of line and then twirl it round your head like a cowboy with a lasso, before letting go at just the right moment so it flies into the water. It's a technique that needs some practice—preferably away from other people to begin with—but once mastered, it can propel your bait a long way. Just remember to make sure the knot tying the end of the line to the can or bottle is a good one, or you'll lose the lot! Once the weight has taken the bait to the bottom, retrieve it in small jerks to attract the fish. To be on the safe side and avoid cuts or burns from the line you should wear gloves.

water, others to flash along at a middle depth—because, depending on conditions, some tactics will work better than others.

Remember that if you're fishing in fresh water there will almost certainly be restrictions on what you can and can't keep, and it's up to you to find out what these are. Fish that fall outside the regulations should be unhooked gently and returned to the water. If in doubt, an adult should do this. There may also be times of the year when you're not allowed to fish at all. In the sea it's often less clear what you're allowed to take for the pot, but again it's up to you to find out. Remember, for example, that spearfishing for certain species may not be permitted.

Going All Tom Sawyer

At least once, you should have a go at fishing the old-fashioned way, with tackle you make or find yourself. You can still use "proper" fishing line and a hook, but everything else can be cobbled together. In the old days, you'd strip a living branch of bendy wood like willow and use that, but in these conservation-minded times, it's best to use something that's fallen already—it won't have the same whip, but it'll do the job. Tie the line to the top of the pole, cut a small piece from a wine-bottle cork and make a hole in it, thread the line through, and tie a hook to the other end—and you're ready to go. For bait, use something from the larder like bread or cheese, or, if you're feeling more daring, you can dig up some worms. You'll also do well with the larger insects like grasshoppers and crickets. Alternatively, in the sea, small pieces of fish make good bait—if you can catch the small fish to begin with!

Don't let very young kids fish on their own. If they're lucky enough to catch something; they're much more likely to damage the fish—and even if you intend to eat it, you should always treat your catch humanely and kill it quickly and efficiently. If the fish is going back into the water, then that requires unhooking, which is something that little fingers aren't always good at.

Watching Wildlife

This isn't just for the kids. Adults can get a real kick out of seeing birds, fish, and animals up close from an entirely different perspective. Boats are perfect for approaching an area stealthily and, more importantly, can get you to places that are simply unreachable on foot. It's also something you can spend as much or as little time on as you like.

Everything's on Your Doorstep

The great thing about watching wildlife from a boat is that there's so much of it—and it nearly all comes to you. Animals and birds are programmed to seek out water, so there's nearly always something going on, and if it's not always as spectacular as seeing a bear come down to the lake's edge

An approach by water is often quieter and allows the chance to see timid creatures.

for a drink, or dolphins racing you out of the bay, it can still be rewarding. It's a great way to spot fish on clear rivers (whether you want to catch them or not), or to see nesting birds (eagles, puffins, herons, cormorants)—and all you need is a pair of binoculars, a digital camera (get one with an optical, rather than a digital zoom), and a logbook to record what you see.

Early mornings are the best times to see wildlife, especially on the shore. It's great for young kids because it helps them to learn the patience that's required to wait for something to happen, and that silence encourages it to happen more quickly.

It's probably a good idea to take along some kind of wildlife encyclopedia so that you can identify anything you see more easily; and a good reference book may also help you to understand why a particular animal is behaving in a particular way. Remember, if you're keen to see something out of the ordinary, talk to the locals; there may be wildlife tours in the area, and tour leaders will know the best spots to visit in order to find the animals you're interested in.

Watching with Care

One of the pleasures of watching wildlife from a boat is that it can allow you to enjoy the company of large mammals that would otherwise avoid you like the plague, or put themselves in such inaccessible places that you can't get near them in the first place. However, although creatures like dolphins, porpoises, and seals are large, they are also highly sensitive, so you need to take special care. For example:

• Keep your distance; approximately 300 ft is good.
• Don't steer your boat directly toward them.
• Make slow and deliberate maneuvers, rather than dodging around to get a better look; slow down gradually rather than coming to a sudden stop.
• Don't touch the animals, don't feed them, and don't try and swim with them.
• Dolphins and porpoises who are swimming with their young are especially sensitive; seals that appear to be resting placidly on the shore may be nursing their young in the breeding season, and won't appreciate it if you get too close.
• Don't make any unnecessary noise, play a radio, or listen to your stereo, no matter how much you might want a "movie moment."
• Remember that messing with animals is probably an offense, so always err on the side of caution. Never attempt to help an injured animal; instead, summon professional help.

Safety First

Don't get so bound up in watching wildlife that you neglect your own safety or the safety of others on the boat. This is particularly true if you're off somewhere remote, or on water that has a strong flowing current, if darkness is falling, or if the weather is turning for the worse. On the other side of the coin, a boat is a very safe way to get closer to large animals that might otherwise be too dangerous to approach. Obviously, you still need to be cautious when getting near anything wild, but it's safer to watch a bear if you're 100 ft away in a canoe than it is if you're the same distance away on foot. Apart from that, the usual rules apply: don't approach any wild animal and don't let the kids wander off animal-watching on their own. And although it shouldn't need saying, don't go whale-watching in your own boat. Whales are large, powerful, unpredictable creatures, and apart from all the marine laws you'll be breaking, you also run the risk of breaking your neck!

Measuring Wind Speed

This is a bit of fun for the kids. It won't let them measure the speed of the wind with any degree of accuracy, but it will show them when the wind is blowing and help them to understand how important wind is to sailors.

All you need is four plastic or paper party cups, a large felt-tipped pen, stapler, ruler, big push pin, scissors, pencil with an eraser on it, two strips of cardboard, and a watch that can display seconds—one of the adults on the boat is bound to have one of these.

Mark one of the cups with the felt-tipped pen so you can tell it apart from the others. Cross the cardboard strips, staple them together, and then staple the cups onto the ends of each arm so that they're all pointing in the same direction. Drive the large push pin through the middle of the cross, then take the eraser end of the pencil and push that into the pin. That will keep the whole thing secure, but still allow it to spin round while someone holds the pencil.

Keep an eye on the marked cup as it spins, and with the help of a watch with a second hand you should be able to work out how many times a minute the device rotates. Over time this will allow you to estimate the wind speed. Congratulations: you've made an anemometer.

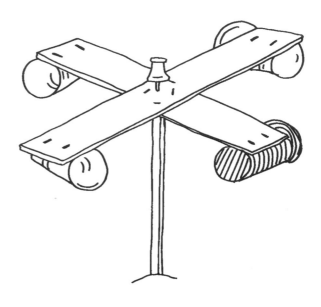

What's the Weather Like?

If you've got young kids, you can turn them into amateur weather forecasters with a few simple bits and pieces. On lakes, rivers, and canals, make sure you keep a lookout for pine cones when you're out walking. These excellent natural forecasters will respond to changes in humidity by opening when it's likely to be wet and closing when it's going to be dry. On salt water, your alternative is seaweed, which behaves in the same way. Basically, moisture in the air causes it to absorb and expand, while dry air will make it crinkle and contract. In fact, you can use almost any kind of marine algae for this—it doesn't have to be seaweed. The traditional way to use seaweed is to nail it to a piece of wood so it hangs down, but you'd better check with the boat's owner first!

Making a Telescope

Being on a boat gives you a unique opportunity to look at life and the world around you from a different perspective. We've said before that boats are great for watching wildlife from, but although you can use a boat to get closer to animals than might be otherwise possible, you may still have to work at a distance. That's where a telescope comes in.

Although a telescope traditionally looks like a tube with a lens at either end, it doesn't always have to be made like that. In fact, you can even make a very basic telescope simply by placing one lens to your eye and then holding the other one in line with it, just in front, and then slowly moving the second lens away from the first until the thing you're looking at swims into focus.

What kind of lenses should you use? The lens that you focus with, sometimes called the "objective" lens, should be convex (in other words, fatter in the middle) and as thin as you can find without it being too fragile; this will make your telescope more powerful. The lens that you look through, sometimes called the eyepiece, can be either convex or concave (in other words, thinner in the middle), and is typically smaller.

Telescopes that use convex eyepieces will show the image upside down in the lens, and are called "Newtonian telescopes," after Sir Isaac Newton; those eyepieces which use convex lenses show things the right way up and are called "Galilean telescopes," after the Italian astronomer Galileo. You can buy lenses from special

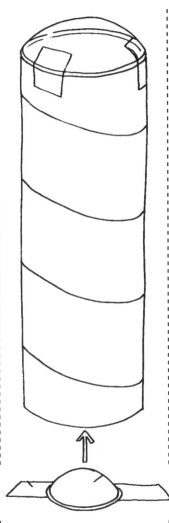

Although you can use lenses from old eyeglasses, you'll get better results from a special optical supplier.

Telescope Safety?
Remember never to look at the sun through a simple telescope. This can cause permanent eye damage, even blindness.

optical shops, or keep a look out for old pairs of spectacles at yard sales and use the lenses from those.

If you want to make the telescope actually look like a telescope, you'll need a cardboard tube—something like a packing tube used to send posters through the mail—so that you can tape a lens to each end. Remember that you should look through the smaller of the two lenses to see the image properly—if there's not a marked difference between them, use a felt-tipped pen to mark a circle around the end with the eyepiece so you know which end is which.

SECTION SIX

Swimming

Of all the activities you can pursue from a boat, swimming is one of the most varied and one of the most enjoyable. Whether it's splashing around and causing a ruckus while jumping off an inflatable dinghy in the local lake, or "proper" diving in a quiet coastal bay, swimming has it all—and it's a wonderful, low-impact exercise that's kind to aging joints and well known for its therapeutic value.

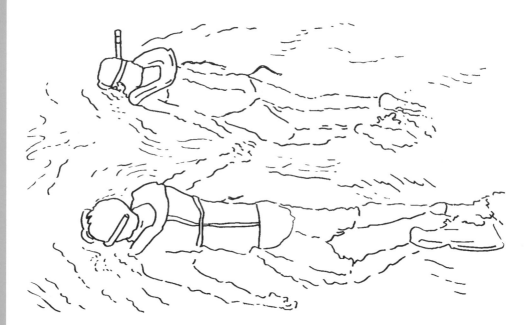

Learn How to Swim

Although personal flotation devices make everyone feel safer on a boat, there's no substitute for being able to swim. You don't need to be the world's strongest swimmer, but you do need confidence in your own ability to stay afloat, and it's important to feel comfortable in the water. Most local sports and leisure centers offer lessons for all ages, so even if it's something you've never learned before—or let's be honest, avoided—you can usually find a class that's teaching people of your own age and ability (i.e. none); the days of a single adult in a class of kids are long gone. It's an important skill, lots of fun, and great exercise, so book a lesson today. (Lessons are good for the simple reason that the swimming style of most people is something they've developed unconsciously over the years, and is usually full of little ticks and quirks that you don't necessarily want to learn!)

Snorkeling and Diving

• Snorkeling gives you the chance to get a proper fish's-eye view of the world below, and can be learned after an hour or two of instruction. Good spots are those with clear water,

Safety First (Again)

- One of the reasons you're not allowed to swim in a marina is probably less obvious than the others: boats that are plugged into an AC current can seep electricity into the water, enough to give you a nasty thump.
- Make sure the boat's geared up for swimming: minimize the slipperiness of the decks, cover sharp objects with an old T-shirt or towel, make sure you can climb back into the boat easily; remember that if you're wearing swim fins, everything is ten times more difficult!
- Make sure the location is geared up for swimming: sharp rocks or coral are no-no's, and if you're planning to dive off the boat, make sure the water's deep enough first.
- Make sure the boat's securely at anchor—a boat can drift faster than you can swim.
- Little bobbing heads in the water are hard to see, while boats are easy to see; swim near your boat so that other water users will steer clear of you.

minimal currents, and where there's something to see like fish or coral. Be careful to disturb neither, and don't try and come away with a chunk of coral as a souvenir—these are delicate, endangered ecosystems. Unless you're messing about in very shallow water, you should always try and snorkel with a friend or "buddy."

• Scuba Diving

(which stands for "self-contained underwater breathing apparatus") is not something you can teach yourself. The equipment is complex and delicate, the techniques are not necessarily very intuitive, and there are many unexpected challenges that can't be overcome without expert tuition, so don't even think about it—this is not a sport where you can borrow a friend's gear and "have a go." However, there are plenty of courses and diving holidays where you can learn about and enjoy this wonderful sport to the full.

There are far too many issues surrounding scuba diving to go into here, but one deserves a mention. There are recognized flags that should be displayed whenever someone is diving, to warn off other water users; this is an important part of any safety routine and should always be observed when there's a diver in the water.

Afraid of the Water?

You'd be amazed how many sailors are actually afraid of the water. Of course, this introduces an unpleasant dynamic for people who love to mess about in boats but who are troubled insistently by their fears. Humans aren't natural swimmers, and that's why a man or woman who can't swim will thrash about if you throw them into the water—they panic. Babies can't swim either, yet if popped into water will exhibit no fear at all. This is because we learn how to be afraid of things as we develop. Try to understand and come to terms with the fear, and you'll be well on the way to conquering it. And take some swimming lessons; there are plenty of people in the same boat. If you'll pardon the expression.

Ghost Stories, Sea Shanties, and Games

Water—and the sea in particular—has been a constant source of inspiration for those trying to frighten the living daylights out of people, and there's no better way to while away the hour before bedtime than with a few ghost stories. After that, you can raise the spirits with a lively sea shanty.

Ghost Ships

There's plenty of fun to be had with tales of some of the famous "specter ships" that have passed into the mythology of sailing and the sea, such as the Flying Dutchman, seen by George, Prince of Wales, off the Australian coast: "a phantom ship, all aglow." Then there's the Mary Celeste, the archetypal ghost ship, discovered adrift in the Atlantic Ocean, 600 miles west of Gibraltar, with plenty of food and fresh water, a broken ship's clock and compass, but no sign of the crew. Details such as the mess table being laid for breakfast with fresh tea brewing were actually added by the author Sir Arthur Conan Doyle, in a short story so realistic that it was published as truth by some newspapers. Still, you can retell the story adding your own details (an alien abduction, a sea monster, a giant whirlpool, or whatever takes your fancy).

Haunted Seas

The Bermuda Triangle sits at the top of this particular spooky list, courtesy of its longevity (Christopher Columbus noted "strange dancing lights" in 1492) and the sheer number of disappearances of boats and planes over the years. Aliens, time warps, sea monsters, take your pick—and don't forget to add in the Formosa Triangle, the Devil's Sea off the coast of Japan, and, of course, the Sargasso Sea.

Pets

Dogs and cats do surprisingly well on board, so long as there's room for them to move about, plenty of warm places to sleep—that's the cats—and you're prepared to make some adjustments. For example, you may have to carry a dog up and down the companionway unless it's got carpet, and even then you may have to knock a couple of planks together for the dog to go up and down. It may also be advisable to harness the little fella when you're not in doggy-paddle distance from the shore, or restrict movement to certain parts of the boat, for example down below. Toilet training is best carried out when a dog is small, and a litter tray seems to have a better than average success rate; though it would be tempting fate to say that any method is foolproof.

Any pet will need a bit of acclimatizing, so try them on short trips first, and take along a favorite toy, blanket, or basket to help them settle in. It's also a good idea to get them some kind of tag that has your details, a note of any permanent mooring, the name of your boat, and so on.

Props

To augment your ghost stories, you'll need some props. While you're spinning a spectral tale, get the kids to close their eyes (or gently blindfold them if they can't be trusted) and then pass round any of the following at relevant times in the story:

• For eyeballs that popped out when the ghost appeared, use peeled grapes.
• For the dead man's hand found still holding the ship's wheel, use a rubber glove filled with water and frozen.

• For the mutineer's guts, torn out by a shark when he jumped from the ship to escape the captain's wrath, use that old favorite, cold spaghetti.
• For his liver, which was sliced out of him before being nailed to the bung hole, use Jell-O®.
• For his brains, which were used to cook up the scurvy plot, use cauliflower (and for his brains which were cooked by headhunters before being shrunk and put on a stick, use broccoli).
• A piece of hot dog for his nose, nutshells for toenails . . . let your imagination run wild.

Sea Shanties

These are songs that were originally sung by sailors to make the time pass more quickly when they were working (usually at some tough, repetitive job). So, "What shall we do with the drunken sailor?" has lines in it like "Hoist him aboard with a running bowline" and "Put him in the scuppers with a hosepipe on him," and so on; while the chorus, "Way, hey, and up she rises," was sung by the men when they were raising the anchor. Use the tune of "Drunken Sailor" to create your own shanties when you want the kids to do chores around the boat: "Force him to wash all the dishes, boys" or "Empty all the heads with a mop and bucket"… you get the idea.

Celestial Navigation

Why would you want to know how to navigate by the stars when you've got a GPS unit and all the technology that a modern boat can offer? Partly because things can go wrong or break down, and partly because if you're any kind of sailor, you just want to know how this stuff works. And that's reason enough to find out a bit more about it.

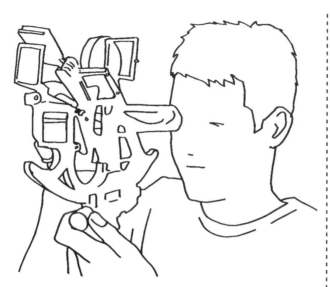

How Does It Work?
- You have to point the sextant at a particular celestial object, for example the sun or a bright star. (Sextants have filters to prevent your eyes being damaged by direct sunlight.)
- Then you adjust the sextant until the object appears to be "sitting" on the horizon and note down the amount you had to turn the knob. (How can you move the sun? It's all down to the way the sextant's mirrors and lenses are arranged.)
- Once you've got that figure, you need to note it down quickly, because waiting only a few seconds can put you out by a nautical mile.
- Next, you check the Nautical Almanac, a book of tables

What Is Celestial Navigation?
Basically, it's a way of using the sun and the stars to find out where you are. In order to do this you need three things:
- A sextant, which is a device that measures the angle of the sun or one of 56 other stars (chosen for their brightness and their distribution in the sky) above the horizon.
- A marine chronometer, essentially a watch that continues to work on a ship; this may sound pretty basic, but the most accurate early timepieces typically used pendulums, which simply didn't work on boats because of the way they roll.

- A current Nautical Almanac, which contains the positions of all the relevant celestial bodies around the year.

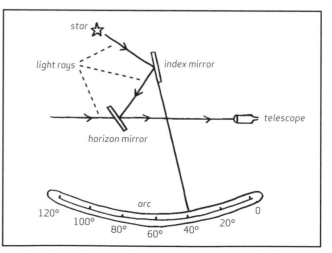

A Little History

For years, sailors used the sun and stars to go from east to west, or vice versa, along a line of latitude. This was fine up to a point, and many times they eventually bumped into one piece of land or another. However, there was no way of establishing a longitude until someone invented a clock that worked properly at sea and which—used in conjunction with a Nautical Almanac—allowed sailors to establish their local time relative to Greenwich mean time. Since the sun moves 15° an hour, it's then possible to work out your longitude from that.

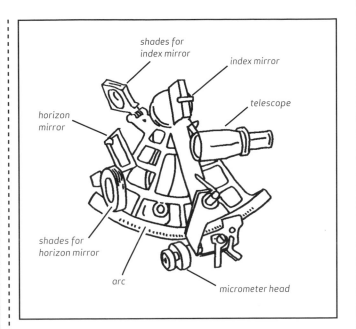

shades for index mirror

index mirror

telescope

horizon mirror

shades for horizon mirror

arc

micrometer head

which lists the exact position of each of those 57 celestial bodies at every time of day.

- You'll then have to go through a series of corrections to take into account instrument error, refraction, and other unavoidable factors.
- Next, it's necessary to check through a second set of tables to confirm the name of the celestial body, its vertical angle (in degrees, minutes, and seconds), and when you took the measurement; this allows you to plot your position.
- You can't use a sextant on cloudy days, because you have to be able to see the sun and/or stars.
- The best time to use a sextant is at dawn or dusk, because then you can see both the celestial bodies and the horizon more clearly (though modern sextants have a way of creating a false horizon if you can't see the real one).
- Sextants are designed for right-handed people.

But I Can't Afford a Sextant

A typical sextant is an expensive piece of equipment—even second-hand, it's likely to cost more than most people will want to spend on something that may end up only being used rarely. However, by scouring the Internet we've found one for less than $20.00. True, it's made of laminated cardboard and you have to build it yourself, but the manufacturer claims that it has an accuracy of "better than eight minutes of arc," which is certainly enough to give you a better-than-ballpark indication of where you are. It includes full instructions for building and using the sextant, as well as an almanac of the sun. And where there's one cardboard sextant, you can bet there are others.

- The Unpredictable
  Elements
- Mechanical Trouble
- Getting Lost
- Help!

SECTION SEVEN

Pitfalls and Problems

The Unpredictable Elements

The weather and the sailor are uneasy friends, particularly if the sailor is actually in a sailboat (as opposed to a boat that relies on an engine or paddles). Then, you want the wind to blow, but you want it to blow to suit you and your course—and the wind doesn't always care to oblige. And then there's the rain, fog, and the various other tricks that the weather has hidden up its capacious, soggy sleeves. Unpredictable indeed.

Be Prepared

The key to having a good time on the water—no matter what kind of water it is—is to be able to anticipate what the weather is going to do next. That starts before your trip, when you should consult whatever weather forecasting services are available to you. Fortunately, today's sailor has more resources than ever before:

• Traditional news outlets have had a love affair with the weather for years, and with more and more local TV and radio stations getting air time, they've got to fill it with something.... Local weather reporting is up to date and reliable and doesn't need any specialist equipment—you can check it from your motel room, or in the car on the way to the lake. If you're traveling any distance, remember that the weather can change in the space of an hour's car journey, and the bright sunny day that greeted you as you pulled out of the driveway may have become damp and foggy by the time you get where you're going.

• The Internet has an extraordinary array of free weather services. If you know where to look, you can find not just up-to-the-minute reports for a specific area, but also long-range forecasts for entire regions (though many weather forecasters believe that the planet's weather system is so unpredictable that a ten-day forecast is at best only 50 percent reliable). You don't have to do anything clever either: just check the weather sites in the "resources" section at the back of the book, and they can lead you on to other websites that have all the information you need. A quick hunt through the top ten sites there should yield something, or lead you on to other websites that have the information you need. Remember, too, that most weather sites display more than one kind of map, so check to see if they've got any information that's specifically for boating enthusiasts, because it'll include more of what you're interested in.

• If your boat is equipped with VHF radio, then you can tune to special weather channels which constantly update their

forecast for the area you're in, allowing you to monitor what's going on and make early, good decisions about what to do. Remember that the weather can change frequently and rapidly, and that the key to using weather information well is to act on it in a decisive and timely fashion. Weather forecasts for water users differ from land-based ones because they take other factors into account, such as wind direction and speed, fog warnings, and so on.

What to Watch Out For

In the general course of things a well-maintained boat and crew—even if there's only one of you—should be able to cope with run-of-the-mill weather. In other words, you may get cold and wet, but not much more so than you would on dry land. But there are specific situations that you need to be aware of at sea that will make all the difference between mild discomfort and genuine unpleasantness. So, assuming you and your boat are prepared for bad weather, here's what you need to look out for:

• Changing Air Pressure

Broadly speaking, if the air pressure is high or going up, then all is well and you're in for a period of settled weather with a low chance of rain. If the pressure drops or is low, then you need to prepare yourself and the boat for unpleasant weather, with clouds and a good chance of persistent rain. Most serious sailors will take a barometer with them; this is the recognized instrument for measuring air pressure.

• What the Clouds Are Doing

High, wispy clouds are called *cirrus*, and are a sign of good weather; cotton-wool clouds are *cumulus* and mean the same, unless "stacked;" then they can form *cumulonimbus* storm clouds. Even layers of cloud are called *stratus*; if they're dark they can indicate persistent, but not necessarily heavy, rain, and if they're light it means fair weather.

• What the Wind Is Doing

Changes in the wind can mean that "new" weather is on the way. In the northern hemisphere this generally means from the west; in the southern hemisphere, weather tends to come from the east. If the wind picks up speed in the opposite direction to any current, it may cause a swell, and in extreme circumstances the waves can swamp the boat.

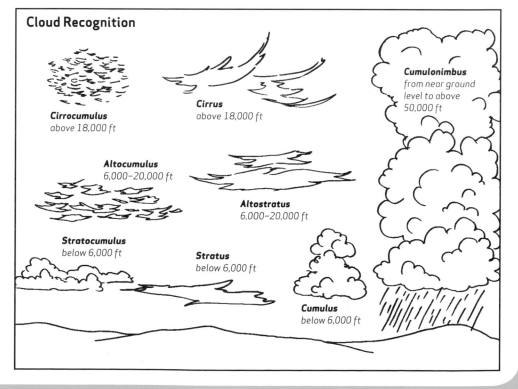

Cloud Recognition

Cirrocumulus
above 18,000 ft

Cirrus
above 18,000 ft

Cumulonimbus
from near ground level to above 50,000 ft

Altocumulus
6,000–20,000 ft

Altostratus
6,000–20,000 ft

Stratocumulus
below 6,000 ft

Stratus
below 6,000 ft

Cumulus
below 6,000 ft

Mechanical Trouble

All boats are machines. They may be as old-fashioned as a wooden canoe or as space-age as a Kevlar® kayak; they may be complex, like a single-person sailboat, or powered by sophisticated engines, like a modern motor cruiser. But if they've got parts, they've got things that can go wrong.

An Ounce of Prevention...

...is worth a pound of cure, so the saying goes; so it'll be no surprise to hear that we recommend you keep your craft in fighting shape by looking after it properly. That means maintenance. Boats are just like cars in that they respond well to being looked after and kept clean; if they use stuff that needs replacing (like oil and antifreeze), then keep an eye on it and replace it in good time. No one likes doing the boring jobs when they could be out enjoying the boat, but always remember that it's much easier to ensure your boat doesn't break down, than to fix it if it does.

The obvious thing to do is to get to know your boat, to listen to her moods and understand what's going on. If something starts behaving oddly—or just differently— make a point of investigating it by either returning to shore early or arriving early next time you want to go out. Ninety percent of the time there won't be anything wrong at all, but in the other ten percent of cases what you discover will be enough to prevent a breakdown. Explore your boat. Find out where the pipes and cables run, check the equipment, look for leaks and anything else that shouldn't be happening, and fix it before it becomes a problem.

Engine Failure

Fifty percent of mechanical problems are down to the engine, so if your boat hasn't got one, good for you. If it has, then the first thing you should do before you take it out is to run a proper restart check to make sure all is well. Your Coast Guard or equivalent service may

well be able to provide you with a checklist you can go through; it will probably look something like this:

- Check the engine mounts for cracks or breaks, and look to see if any other fittings appear in poor condition; then check belts and hoses for the same.
- While you're there, look for leakage around the hoses and gaskets, and check to see if there's any oil in the bilge; if there is, it could be leaking from the engine.
- Check the oil level, and make sure the oil itself isn't milky, because that's one of the signs that water has got into the engine at some point.
- Look for white residue on the engine, which can indicate that it is running too hot.
- Are the spark plugs worn or burnt?

Other Considerations
Although the majority of your problems are going to be engine-related, there are plenty of other things to go wrong on a boat:

- Regularly check the sails, rigging, ropes, and all the hardware on your sailboat.
- Open and close hatches—you'll be especially glad that they close properly if you hit some rough weather.
- Examine electrical connections for any signs of rust.
- When you can, do a thorough check of the hull while the boat's out of the water. Look for stress cracks, chipping, cracks in the gel coat, blisters on the hull, and any other bumps and bruises.
- Check the condition of the rudder and tiller, and the centerboard or daggerboard if you have one.

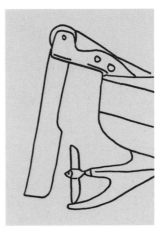

- Check that your boat's batteries are firmly secured and sit properly in their acid-proof containers.
- Check your fuel tanks and lines—use your nose as well as your eyes.

Your Boating Toolbox
Although it's possible to buy a boating toolkit, many of the tools are the same as the ones you'd buy in a decent auto shop. The one thing the toolbox may have going for it is that it should be waterproof and float. You can fill it with an assortment of wrenches, Phillips-head and flat-blade screwdrivers, a couple of hammers, needle-nose pliers, vise grips, and wire cutters—and check to see if anything needs a hex wrench (Allen key); if it does, pack one with multiple sizes. Just as important, you need to carry spares for important components like hoses, belts, spark plugs, and fuses, electrical and duct tape, a selection of those plastic zip ties, spare water, and oil.

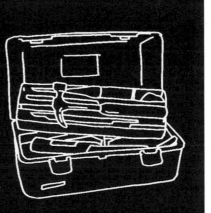

SECTION SEVEN

Getting Lost

Some people can get lost on a cruise ship as they make their way from the stateroom to the restaurant; others can find their way across the Atlantic on their own, or over Lake Superior in a dead fog. The trick is preparedness, and becoming familiar with the sailor's worst enemy—your own limitations.

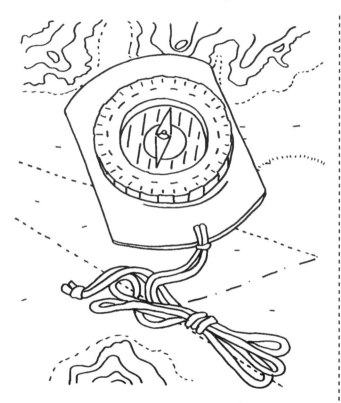

If you've moved further off the beaten track and are, for example, kayaking along a river for a few days in search of wild trout, then you've hopefully brought a compass and a proper topological map with you (rather than just a cell phone which will almost certainly not work beyond a certain point); just as important, you'll know how to use them. If you're stuck on land, as it were, out in the wilderness, then there are several easy tricks you can try to find out where you are, and we'll talk about these in the box entitled "Lost Inland."

What Works in Your Favor

- You filed a float plan so someone responsible knows where you're supposed to be and when you're supposed to return; when you don't, they'll sound the alarm.

The simple fact of the matter is that if you know what you're doing and you've prepared properly, then you will rarely get lost. You may misplace yourself for a short while, but that's not the same thing at all—not knowing quite where you are as you come into a large bay, looking for where you parked the car, isn't the same thing as being stone-cold lost in the middle of a massive lake, where the shores are so far away that you can't see them—or being caught out in an actual, real ocean.

Many sailors will never get lost, at least not in any real sense. Pottering along on a canal boat or in a canoe, or cruising up a river in a little family motorboat and not sure where you are? What on earth will you do? Oh, right: stop and ask someone. And while you're about it, moor up and have a snack in a riverside inn.

Lost Inland

So, you've boated off into the middle of nowhere and are well and truly lost. Here's what you can do:

- Admit you're lost. This prevents you from just crashing off in a random direction because you feel you should be "doing something," and getting more lost.
- Apply the STOP principle: Sit, Think, Observe, Plan. Try and work out the last time you knew where you were, and use your map, if you have one.
- If you've been on a river, all you need to do is find your way back and then follow it downstream until you hit civilization.
- If you can get up high without making things worse (i.e. getting more lost), then have a look for any recognizable landmarks.
- Otherwise, stay put until someone finds you.

- You have navigational aids that you know how to use, including a nautical map, compass, GPS, and the other tools necessary to work out where you are and plot a course to safety.
- You've kept a proper ship's log and are thus able to work out your position using dead reckoning (see page 67) should all of the electronic devices on the boat conk out at the same time.
- You have the requisite lights to display should you remain lost as darkness falls.
- You have visual and audible signals that you can let off to attract attention, such as flares, flags, lights, and foghorns.

What Works Against You

- You didn't do any of the stuff in the previous section.
- You've got flares and lights and sound-making devices but you don't know how or when to use them.
- You don't know how to work your radio properly.
- You don't take steps to remove yourself and the boat from immediate danger—for example, you may not know where you are, but if there are lots of very large boats about it's likely you're too near a shipping lane.
- You panic and make the situation worse by not paying attention to what's going on around you, swamping the boat by making erratic moves, moving heedlessly toward more dangerous water.
- You try to move at night, when waiting for daylight may be all that's required to reorient and make yourself and the boat safe.

If you think you're lost, stay put. Remember: your boat is much easier to see from the air than you are.

Help!

OK, even the best-prepared, most careful, conscientious sailor can run into difficulties through no fault of their own. They can be pretty serious difficulties, too, and over the next few pages we'll look at some of the biggies, including running aground, capsizing, sinking, and catching fire. In certain circumstances, all of these are serious enough to be classed as emergencies, and it's important to understand what steps you can take to sort yourself out.

Running Aground

This is what happens when the bottom of your boat meets the bottom of the lake, river, or sea when, moments before, you were skimming along and not paying very much attention. There are various degrees of running aground, depending on the different factors involved, but two crucial components dictate how serious it is: the speed the boat is traveling at when it hits, and the physical make-up of the bottom itself. It's possible, for example, to come to the gentlest of stops on a sandbank without causing any damage at all; but then again you can whack into razor-sharp rocks and rip out half the bottom of the boat before you know what's hit you.

• How to Avoid It

Learn how to read a chart properly, so you can avoid shallow water and not get into this trouble in the first place. Understand your boat as well as you can: how deep the rudder and centerboard go (and thus how deep your draft is), how to raise them quickly if you need to, how to tell the depth of the water around you either visually or by using a depth sounder.

• How to Deal with It

If you're fortunate enough to have run slowly into sand and you're alert, it may be possible just to steer straight back out again. If not, get the sails down if you have them, as this will stop you being pushed further aground. Got a centerboard?—pull it up fast. Try rocking the boat to one side to reduce the draft (this is called "heeling"), and if you can, get someone to check the bilges to make sure you're not taking on water. If the rudder isn't stuck, you may be able to reverse off with your engines. To reduce your draft, try getting rid of any heavy objects by dumping them into a dinghy. Set the anchor, and either try and use it to pull yourself off, or wait and see if the tide will float you off. Only take a tow as a last resort, in case the boat is damaged by being pulled off the rocks.

Getting Rescued

If you've called out a lifeboat, the skipper will want to talk to you to find out the current situation, so keep your radio on if possible. It's going to be confusing on the boat, but try and make sure that there aren't any loose lines in the water around that may foul the lifeboat's propeller when it comes in close. Remember that the lifeboat has a single priority, and that's to get people safely off the boat; it's not a salvage vessel, though it will offer a tow if it's able to.

If a helicopter arrives, you'll need to keep the radio on for as long as possible. Helicopters make a fantastic amount of noise, and you won't be able to hear much of anything with one hovering overhead. The pilot will ask you to steer a steady course if you can, and will then usually send down a weighted line, which needs to drop into the water to earth itself first; then you can gather the end, but don't secure it. The helicopter will send down one of the crew and they'll take things from there.

Radio for Help

You can use Channel 16 on your VHF radio to call for help from the Coast Guard. Give them the name of your boat, its position, how many people are on the boat, what's happened, and what assistance you need. Modern VHF radios are equipped with a distress button which you can just press, and that'll send an emergency call. Always use your radio rather than a cell phone, which will have intermittent coverage and will only be able to reach a single person. Inevitably there's an etiquette when using the radio.

If you're in need of assistance, it goes like this:
- You say "Pan pan" (pronounced "pawn") three times, followed by "All ships" three times, followed by "This is [say the name of your boat]" three times.
- Then you give the MMSI (Maritime Mobile Service Identity) if you have one, and your position.
- Then you summarize your current situation.
- Finish each transmission with "Over."

If your life is immediate danger, it goes like this:
- Say "Mayday" three times, followed by "This is [the name of your boat]" three times, followed by "Mayday" and the name of your boat, once.
- Then you give the MMSI if you have one, and your position.
- Then you summarize your present situation and give the number of people on board ship.
- Finish each transmission with "Over."

SECTION SEVEN

Help! continued

Capsizing

This is what happens when your boat tilts over so far that it goes onto its side and starts to ship water; in extreme circumstances, it will actually "turn turtle" and go completely upside down. Though this is potentially unpleasant and awkward, the design of modern boats makes them easier to right than ever before, and if your gear is stowed away properly, you may not even lose anything. The ease with which you can right a capsized boat depends on the type of boat. A modern dinghy, for example, is designed to drain water really quickly, and sits high in the water so it's easier to get back up. A catamaran, on the other hand, can be a real pain, since you've got to manhandle the mast, the rigging, and any associated

Modern dinghies are designed so that the water drains away quickly, making them easier to right.

hardware, plus the hull that's tipped over its vertical axis; in fact, the chances of a solo sailor being able to right anything but the tiniest catamaran without help are pretty slim.

• How to Avoid It

Buy an inflatable or a canal boat or a motor cruiser, because they're either impossible or really, really hard to capsize. Otherwise, keep an eye on the wind and

bet will almost certainly be to stay with the boat, and here are the reasons why:

- It's likely to help you to stay afloat; indeed, you may even be able to climb onto it while you wait for help.
- Assuming you got off a radio message with your position, people are going to come looking for you, and your boat is a lot easier to see bobbing in the water than you are, so stay close to it.

If your boat is upside down and drifting, still stay with it, unless it's clearly drifting into danger; if there's more than one of you, stick together.

Adopt the so-called "HELP" position—Heat Escape Lessening Posture—by pulling your knees into your chest, crossing your feet, crossing your arms over your chest, and letting your personal flotation device do the work. This will help you to retain more body heat (which is vital, because even warm water will leach heat out of your body more quickly than you might think) and relax you so you can conserve energy.

the sails so that your boat doesn't simply blow over, as this is the most common cause of a capsize. Watch for large waves and the wakes of large boats, as these can rock you over. If you're in a canoe or a kayak, then it's hard to capsize in flat, calm water; however, a large unexpected wave, the wake of a thoughtless boat, and human error can all result in a full capsize.

- **How to Deal with It**
If you've got a sailboat with a centerboard, you've got the opportunity to climb gracefully up onto the gunwale as the boat goes over, before stepping down onto the centerboard. There you can keep everything nice and balanced while you work out what to do next. Resist the natural temptation to throw yourself onto the sail as it goes over; this is really stupid, as you'll more than likely just sink the

mast. If you can't climb over elegantly, then swim around to the centerboard. Before you try and right the boat, loosen the sails—otherwise you're likely to capsize all over again before you can get her up. Righting a canoe when you're still in it is a specialized skill beyond the scope of this book.

Sinking
Should your boat sink, or be impossible to right, then you've got some important decisions to make. Actually, you've got one important decision to make: should you stay with the boat, or try and swim to shore and safety? If you're in a canal, where the water is likely to be still and calm, and the shore close at hand, the easiest solution will be to head for dry land. In almost all other cases, however, your best

Help! continued

stove unattended. If you can't live without candles, make sure they're in sturdy, stable containers, away from draughts and anything else that can catch light; blow them out when you leave the cabin. Use safety matches only, and keep them away from the kids. Don't smoke in bed; better still, don't smoke at all. Clean the bilges regularly of oil residue and other flammable trash. Install alarms that detect smoke, gas, and gasoline vapor.

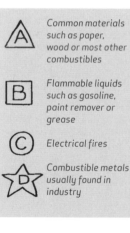

Ⓐ Common materials such as paper, wood or most other combustibles

Ⓑ Flammable liquids such as gasoline, paint remover or grease

Ⓒ Electrical fires

☆ Combustible metals usually found in industry

Fire

Fire on a boat can be a killer. It can cause panic and confusion, and when you add to that a collection of people in a confined space who may not be familiar with the boat or with proper fire procedures, you've got a recipe for disaster. Fortunately, it's possible to take plenty of steps to prevent fires on board.

• **How to Avoid It**
Make a fire action plan so that there's an escape route for every sleeping position. Make sure your routes are usable—that they're not blocked, they're big enough, and hatches open properly (or, if your route involves a window, that there's a readily available means to break it). Everyone needs to run through the route in their heads so that they're confident they know their steps to escape, even in the darkness and confusion of an onboard fire. Turn off appliances when not in use, and NEVER leave a lit

• **How to Deal With It**
Radio for help, and get everyone into a life jacket. Use your extinguishers to put out a small fire, keeping your head low—smoke and fumes kill more people than fire does. If the fire is spreading, give up and get out, closing doors behind you as you go. If you suspect an engine-room fire, don't open the hatch to check, or the increase in oxygen may create a flash fire.

Using a Fire Extinguisher

For those of us who didn't go in for end-of-year horseplay at school (which invariably includes letting off a fire extinguisher or two), how do you actually use one? Easy, just remember **PASS**:

• **P**ull the pin.
• **A**im the extinguisher at the bottom of the flames.
• **S**queeze the trigger on the handle.
• **S**weep the extinguisher back and forth across the base of the fire.

If you're able to, turn off gas cylinders and anything else inflammable. Don't pick up something that's alight in order to throw it overboard—you're just as likely to spread the fire. Never try and put out a deep-fryer fire with an extinguisher, because you'll just splatter burning fat everywhere; extinguish it with a fire blanket instead. Finally, get everyone off the boat and into the water; remember that a fire can reignite even after you think you've put it out.

Person Overboard

Falling overboard can range from an inconvenience to a genuinely life-threatening situation, depending on the circumstances and the person involved. Very few people are injured in the act of falling overboard; most problems arise because they're not wearing a personal flotation device, and/or are unable to get back into the boat.

Solo Sailor Overboard

If you're out alone and you end up in the water, it can be really difficult to get back into the boat. Some larger boats have a platform that you can climb onto, or a ladder, but others have nothing. On a small boat you'll need to try and pull yourself up out of the water to the point at which your chest is partly in the boat, then kick your legs as if you were swimming, and then give a final heave so you kind of tip forward into the boat. But this is exhausting, and not guaranteed to work. Solo sailors should consider carrying a personal light, and a whistle to attract attention. Getting back into a boat on your own is very difficult, and you should spend most of your energies making sure you don't fall out in the first place.

• **How to Avoid It**

Be aware of what's going on around you, so you can anticipate sudden movements in the boat which would otherwise catch you unawares. Practice the idea of "one hand for the boat and one hand for yourself" (i.e. never move around the boat without holding on to something). There's rarely room for horseplay on a boat, and anyone who's had a drink needs to be especially careful. It's good practice to keep decks, companionways, and stairs free from obstructions. When you're standing still, bending your knees will give you better balance.

• **How to Deal with It**

First, shout out to reassure them that you're aware they've fallen in. Next, make sure you keep them in sight the whole time; if you can't, get someone else to do

it—it can be very hard to find someone again in the water once you've lost sight of them. Now turn the boat in the direction in which they fell; this will move the rudder and propeller away from them. Throw them a lifebelt—otherwise known as a Type IV flotation device—aiming slightly upwind and with an underarm action; this will give you more control, and you'll be able to throw it further. Try to approach them by heading into the wind or the waves; this will give you more control over the boat and stop it from drifting into them. When you come alongside, use a combination of the flotation device (which they should be hanging on to) and a boathook to get them on board, keeping nice and low as you do, so they don't overbalance you and pull you in with them.

- First Aid
- Carbon Monoxide
- Useful Knots
- The Beaufort Scale
- Distress Signals
- Glossary of Terms

SECTION EIGHT

References and Resources

First Aid

With any luck—and the proper preparation, of course—your boating trip should proceed without a hitch, leaving you with nothing to do but enjoy yourself. However, from time to time, incidents will occur and accidents will happen. The trick is to be ready for them, to minimize their impact on the trip, and act quickly to make the person concerned safe and comfortable. In the pages that follow we'll look at both the most serious and some of the most common accidents that can occur on board, and consider what to do about them.

Hypothermia

You get cold on a boat. You wouldn't think so, with all that sun and all that exercise, but there's wind and rain too, and if you fall into even a warm sea, you'll be surprised at how cold you can get, and how quickly it can start to cause problems.

• What Is It?

Hypothermia occurs when the body is unable to generate enough heat to compensate for the heat that it's losing. Even a 2°F drop in body temperature (from the usual 98.6°F/37°C) can bring on hypothermia.

• What Happens?

Your body is a little power station that sits there manufacturing heat. If it's cold, or if the wind and rain are leaching that heat away faster than your

When to Get Help

If in doubt, do it straight away. For example, if someone gets into difficulties in the water, climbs out unaided, and seems fine, it's quite possible they could still go into hypothermia. The very best thing you can do for yourself and your crew is to get some first-aid training, learn how to administer important procedures like CPR, and never overstretch yourself. It's always better to be berated for being a killjoy, and cutting a trip short in order to be certain than someone's OK, than to be remembered for something altogether more serious than a missed afternoon on the water. After all, there will always be time for more boat trips.

body can generate it, then hypothermia can set in. It doesn't even have to feel cold.

- **What Can You do About It?** Watch for signs like lethargy, shivering (your body does this automatically to try and make more heat), poor coordination, irritability, and even slurred speech. If the person is in wet clothes, get them into something dry and then keep them out of the wind; make sure you cover their head. The temptation is to chafe their skin to try and warm them up, but this doesn't do any good; instead, you have to reduce any further heat loss with the dry clothes and then let the body get back to generating heat, which is the quickest way out of the situation. Give them something easy to eat that will release calories quickly, like an energy bar; give them water or a warm, sweet drink. Do not give them alcohol. If the person does not recover quickly, or gets worse, make for shore and seek medical help. Severe hypothermia is a life-threatening condition and needs to be treated by a professional as soon as possible.

Near-Drowning
When you're surrounded by water, it's probably inevitable that at some point during your boating life, either you or someone you're with will

Treating Burns
There are basically three kinds of burns: first-, second-, and third-degree. First-degree burns are barely distinguishable from the scalds caused by hot coffee, or the kind of thing you'll get from being out in the sun. Second-degree burns occur if the skin appears raw and blistered; these are not dangerous unless a large area (more than 50 percent in adults) is affected. Third-degree burns damage not just the skin but also fat, muscles, and nerves, and as a result, the skin may appear charred.

- **Minor burns** should be treated by applying lots of cold water for about 10 minutes; remove anything from the affected area that may constrict it in the event of swelling, and then cover it with a dressing from your first-aid kit. If you don't have anything handy, you can even use a clean plastic food bag.

- **Severe burns** are a different kettle of fish, and there's not really any treatment you can apply. First, there's a danger of shock, particularly if the burns are extensive; second, there's a danger of infection, especially if you burst blisters or further damage the wound. Apply plenty of cold water, then lay the person down and try and make them comfortable, if you can do this without damaging the affected area. If anything is stuck to the burn, your instinct will be to remove it—don't. Summon medical help and/or return to shore immediately. If you suspect shock, try and make the person warm, raise and support their legs, loosen tight clothing, and try to keep them still while you get help.

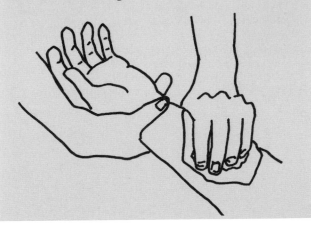

SECTION EIGHT

First Aid continued

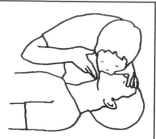

1. Tilt back the head and lift the chin slightly. Look and listen for signs of breathing.

2. If the person is not breathing, cover their mouth with yours, pinch their nose, and blow until you see their chest rise. Do this twice initially.

3. If they're still not breathing, put the heel of one hand on the middle of their chest, and place the other hand on top. Push down about 2 in 30 times. Repeat, giving two breaths then 30 pushes, until the person recovers.

fall in. We've talked through the person-overboard scenario on page 123, but if you find yourself in the extreme situation where you get them back and they're not breathing, you need to use cardiopulmonary resuscitation (CPR).

• What Is It?
You need a constant supply of oxygen, which enters the bloodstream via the lungs. When you start to drown, your air passage closes involuntarily to stop water getting into your lungs; unfortunately, it also stops air going the same way.

What happens next varies, but the result is the same: either the larynx remains closed and "dry" drowning begins, or it relaxes and lets water into the lungs, which causes "wet" drowning. In both cases the result is hypoxemia—an insufficient level of oxygen in the blood.

• What Happens?
Within about three minutes, the victim is unconscious; within five, the brain begins to be starved of

oxygen, the heart may beat very erratically or stop completely, and, depending on the temperature of the water, hypothermia may occur.

• What Can You do About It?
Perform CPR, which has two functions: it gets oxygen into the lungs, and it stimulates the heart. Get the person onto their back, and then tilt their head back to clear the airway. Check to see if their chest is rising and falling, then put your ear to their open mouth and check whether they're breathing. If there's no sign of breath, pinch their nose and take a deep breath, put your mouth over theirs, and blow in so that their chest rises. Repeat once every five seconds, pausing every ten breaths to check for signs of recovery. If they're still not breathing, start compressing the chest. Put the palm of one hand on their chest between their nipples, put the other hand on top, and lace the fingers. Push down firmly to compress the chest by 1–2 in, 15

Sunburn and Worse

One of the most common problems afloat is also one of the easiest to avoid. When you're on a boat you can easily be deceived by the wind, which makes the sun feel less powerful than it actually is; remember that it's perfectly possible to get a bad sunburn on a cloudy day. So, wear a hat with a bill to shield your eyes, and something to cover your neck. And cover up with a high-factor sunscreen to prevent burning. Sunburn can make you feel awful—sick, headachy, and lethargic—and it really hurts! If you're doing a lot of swimming, remember to reapply sunscreen, even if the label says it's waterproof.

times. Stop and do two breaths, then another 15 compressions. Continue until the person recovers. If they show no sign of recovery, seek medical help as soon as possible.

Dehydration

Even sitting at a desk at work, or at home on the weekend, relaxing in the garden or in front of the TV, few of us drink as much water as we ought. Add to this more exercise than you may be used to, and it's quite possible to spend most of your boat trip slightly dehydrated. Mild dehydration won't do you any serious harm, but if it escalates, there could be trouble.

• What Is It?

It's pretty simple, really. Your body is nearly 70 percent water, and if you start to lose more water than you drink, dehydration is the result.

• What Happens?

Symptoms vary. If you're mildly dehydrated and your body is used to it, you may not notice anything at all. Otherwise, the telltale signs are thirst, dry mouth, headaches, irritability, fatigue, and dark urine (or no urine at all). If your body experiences a 5 percent fluid loss, you'll feel all the above symptoms, while at 10 percent you'll get dizzy, find it hard to breathe, and your headache may increase to severe; above 10 percent takes you into the danger zone where you may become delirious. Worse, if you get severely dehydrated, you won't be able to drink anything because your body will reject it—every time you take a drink of water, you'll just throw it back up.

First Aid continued

• **What Can You Do About It?** The best way to deal with dehydration is to drink little and often so that you don't have a problem in the first place. The mistake that people make is to wait until they're thirsty before they take a drink. Don't. You should aim to drink between six and eight pints (3–4 liters) of water a day on a typical sailing trip—that works out at about a cup every half-hour—and remember to replenish any salts you may be losing through sweat. A handful of peanuts or some other high-salt, high-energy snack will do the trick. Remember that some of the drinks you enjoy—like coffee, tea, and most sodas—are actually diuretics and will make you go to the toilet more often than usual, thus dehydrating you more. If you feel that you're slightly dehydrated, you can sort yourself out quickly enough by drinking a cup of water every 15 minutes for the first hour and then reverting to a cup every half-hour after that.

Cuts and Bruises

Bruises are troublesome and can be painful—especially the next day—but they're rarely dangerous. If a bruise is particularly painful or livid, you can often relieve the discomfort a little by raising the affected area to slow the flow of blood, or by dabbing it gently with a facecloth wetted with cold water.

Most cuts don't need any real attention, and will stop bleeding all by themselves. If one is more persistent, you can usually staunch the flow by applying pressure with a bandage or a clean cloth; then gently dab the wound clean to dry it, and apply some antiseptic cream before covering with a dressing. If it's a more serious wound, then try and stop the flow of blood with pressure (take turns if it's hard work, but don't apply a tourniquet unless you know what you're doing, as this can cause more harm than good) while you make for shore and seek medical help.

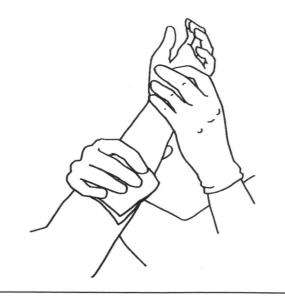

Bites and Stings

Insects love water almost as much as they enjoy chowing down on people, so you'll need to take steps to prevent getting bitten. Although natural repellents like citronella work for some people, DEET-based products are still the most effective— though you should consult with your family doctor before applying them on young kids. Remember to reapply after swimming, and note that the insects' "witching hour" is around sundown.

Carbon Monoxide

This is probably the single most toxic substance you'll come across in your everyday life, and under the right conditions it's a killer—a killer that you can't see, or smell, or taste. That's why it's important to understand what it is, what it does, and how to avoid it.

• **What Is It?**
It's a poisonous gas produced by the incomplete burning of carbon-based fuels—such as gasoline in an engine—that's especially dangerous when it collects unnoticed.

• **What Happens?**
When you breathe it in, carbon dioxide goes into the lungs and displaces the oxygen in the bloodstream. When your body doesn't get the oxygen it needs, the consequences are always serious and can result in death. Common symptoms of carbon monoxide poisoning are problems with your vision, dullness and confusion, headaches, nausea, weakness, and dizziness. Even a short exposure to high levels of carbon monoxide can result in death.

• **Where Is It?**
Since it's produced by the engine, it's going to be in and around there as well as in the exhaust—though because it's heavier than air it will also tend to collect at the bottom of the boat, in the bilges. Serious problems can arise if the exhaust is blocked, because this can result in carbon monoxide collecting elsewhere on the boat, even in the cabin or cockpit; indeed, if there's a boat idling nearby, you should try and stay at least 20 ft away from it. If there's a tailwind, or if you're running with the bow too high in the water, this may cause carbon monoxide to build up.

Easily the most dangerous area is at the stern of the boat, where carbon monoxide can collect around the swim platform; if you think about it, this is a pretty stupid place to encourage people to get in and out of the water, since the propeller is also there, just under the water and out of sight. If people are spending time in the water where an engine is leaking the gas out of the exhaust, then they're in a danger area.

• **What Can You do About It?**
Buy carbon monoxide detectors and take advice about where to put them on your boat. Make sure they work before each trip. Turn off gas bottles when you leave the boat, and use a hand-held carbon monoxide "sniffer" when you come back on board. If you suspect that someone has carbon monoxide poisoning, then move them into fresh air immediately. If you've got oxygen (this is unlikely), administer it. Get them to a medical professional as soon as you can, radioing ahead for help if you suspect their condition is serious.

A hand-held carbon monoxide "sniffer".

Useful Knots

A knot, or a lashing, is the sailor's best friend, and you don't have to be out on an actual sailboat to appreciate that. Knots are everywhere, from tying up at a marina mooring with bow, stern, and spring lines, to hitching a canoe to a handy tree; from heaving that ancient rope around the bollard next to the canal, to tying down that flapping bit of awning over the cockpit in your motor cruiser.

There are literally thousands of knots. In fact, there are enough to fill a whole book. In fact, one day, maybe I'll write that book. In the meantime, though, let's go through some of the sailor's favorite knots in simple, step-by-step fashion, looking at some examples of how the knots are used and talking about how to store and care for rope properly.

Rope Terminology
- **Bight:** any section of rope that is slack or curved, or has a loop in it.
- **Loop:** the circle that is made when you pass the working end of the rope over itself.
- **Standing end:** the end of the rope that does not have a knot in it.
- **Working end:** the part of the rope that you're currently working with.
- **Turn:** the act of taking of a section of rope around the standing part, or around another object such as a ring or a section of wood.

Figure Eight

We're going to start with one of the easiest and most commonly used knots, which is designed as a kind of stop-knot—the idea is to prevent a secured rope from coming loose and then running through any kind of retaining device, for example a pulley. It goes like this:

1. Take the working end of the rope and loop it behind the main length.

2. Hold the loop in place, and then bring the working end back around the front of the main length.

3. If you take the working end down through the loop at this point, you'll end up with a basic overhand knot (probably the first knot you ever tied as a kid)—so don't. Instead, take it behind the loop and then pull it through to form a proper figure-eight knot.

4. Pull both parts to complete the knot, like so.

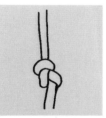

Bowline

The best-loved and most widely used general-purpose knot in sailing. You can use it to fasten a safety line around someone's chest, to attach a line around a bollard, to jerry-rig a bosun's chair or improvise a ladder, and to secure a line to a crossbeam or ring. It has other important characteristics as well: notably that it's easy to undo when you need to, and weakens the rope less than other popular knots like the sheet bend or the reef knot.

1. Take the working end of the rope about 6 in from the end. Then lay the end over the main length of rope to form a cross like this, with a loop below it.

2. Next, take the working end and bring it around the main length of rope, then up through the loop like so.

3. With your other hand, firmly hold the section where the ropes cross over; then take the end of the rope up and out of the loop, and then around the back of the main line again.

4. Bring the working end around the back and then down through the smaller loop, and tighten the knot slowly so that you leave a decent loop in the rope. The loose end should be about 2–3 in long.

 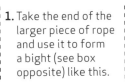 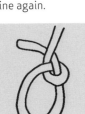 

Sheet Bend

This is a great knot for joining two lines together, especially when those lines are of different diameters. For this reason it's sometimes known as a weaver's hitch. Here goes:

1. Take the end of the larger piece of rope and use it to form a bight (see box opposite) like this.

2. Thread the second, smaller piece of rope under the bight and then carry it over the top of the bight like so.

3. Fold the working end of the smaller piece of rope under the bight that you formed in step 1.

4. Bring the working end over the top of the bight and then under itself, then over the other part of the bight.

5. Finally, pull both parts to tighten and complete the knot.

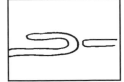  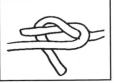 

Useful Knots continued

Anchor Bend

As its name suggests, this is used for tying a rope onto a ring or something similar—an anchor chain, for example—and so finds wide use on boats of all descriptions. It's also sometimes known as the anchor hitch or the fisherman's bend. Here you go:

1. Take the working end of the rope and thread it over the ring once, then once again, so that the working end points in the same direction as the main length of rope.

2. Next, take the working end around the main rope and thread it through the loop, like so.

3. Make sure you've got enough rope left over at the end, and tighten.

4. Finish off by taking the working end around the main line again to form a loop, and then pulling it through that loop and tightening to finish.

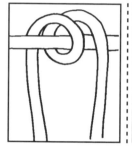 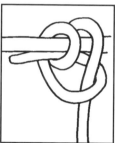 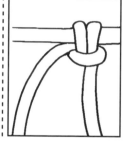 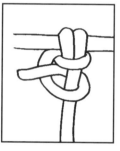

Cleat Hitch

A cleat is typically a metal attachment on a boat, a quay, or a mooring for fastening a rope. The standard design looks a bit like a squashed, extended anvil with two "horns" extending out from a central support. This is not so much a knot as a lashing, and is used all over the world to tie a boat up.

1. Wrap the working end round the cleat once. Bring the end of the rope around the other end of the cleat and then over the top.

2. Thread the rope under the other end of the cleat, then bring it back round and over the top.

3. Form a loop in the working end, then maneuver that over the other end of the cleat.

4. Pull it tight, like so, to complete the lashing.

  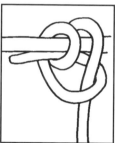 

Storing Rope

Rope that is dumped after use anywhere on the boat immediately becomes a hazard. Even worse, it starts to deteriorate—and for something seemingly so strong and solid, it deteriorates quickly. Given the key role played by rope on most boats, it's important to look after it properly.

You should always coil a rope when it's not being used (though if it's a long piece of rope you can get away with merely coiling the ends); if you don't, then the resulting kinks in the rope will diminish its overall strength. Coil rope using both hands. If you're right-handed, support it with your left hand and bring it round clockwise with your right hand, giving it a gentle but firm twist as you go to flatten it out (a coiled rope that's full of "springs" is no use to anyone). If you're left-handed, reverse the hands and use a counterclockwise coiling motion. Try and make sure the coils are of even length, as this makes them easier to handle and simpler to hang; always hang ropes when you're not using them, rather than laying them on the floor.

To finish off, when you've got about three or four feet of rope left, wrap it around the coil three times, then take the end and turn it into a loop. Push the loop through the gap in the top half of the coil and then slip it over the top. Pull the end tight to help flatten the coil of rope. Some people reckon that braided rope keeps its strength and shape for longer if you coil it into a figure eight, but with modern rope that's looked after properly, that's not necessary. Hang the coiled rope in a dry place.

1. If you are right handed, hold the rope in your left hand and make coils with your right. Twist the rope away from you between thumb and forefinger so that the coils form circles.

2. Finish coiling the rope leaving a long working end. Wrap this several times around the coils to bind them together.

3. Make a loop with the remainder of the working end and push this through the top of the coil, above the binding.

4. Pull the loop over the top of the coil and down to the bound part, then pull the working end to secure it.

You can use the end of the rope to hang the coil when you stow it if you wish. When you need to make the rope ready for use simply hold the coils in your left hand and loosen the binding loop with your right. Lift the binding loop back over the top of the coil then unwrap the binding turns.

SECTION EIGHT

The Beaufort Scale

When it comes to wind speed, sailors all over the world share a common language. It's the language that allows them to distinguish between a light air and a gentle breeze, or a fresh breeze and a strong gale. It was invented in 1805 by an admiral in the British Navy, Sir Francis Beaufort, and it's named after him to this day. Welcome to the Beaufort scale.

Force	Velocity	Description
0	Less than 1 knot	**Calm:** smoke rises straight up in the air and the sea is like a mirror.
1	1–3 knots	**Light air:** gentle ripples form on the surface, but it's easier to tell the wind direction by watching smoke blow across the water.
2	4–6 knots	**Light breeze:** you can feel the wind on your face, a weather vane will turn, short wavelets form on the surface, without crests.
3	7–10 knots	**Gentle breeze:** larger wavelets with some breaking crests, leaves constantly moving in the trees, small flags will blow straight.
4	11–16 knots	**Moderate breeze:** will blow loose paper off the deck and move small branches in the trees; wavelets become longer, with frequent breaking crests.
5	17–21 knots	**Fresh breeze:** moderate waves with plenty of white caps, small trees sway, and wavelets form on inland waters.
6	22–27 knots	**Strong breeze:** large waves with extensive white tops form, the large branches of trees move, telegraph wires hum, hard to open an umbrella.
7	28–33 knots	**Near gale:** white tops aplenty as the sea starts to heave, some even breaking up into the air and being blown by the wind; on land, entire trees move and it becomes awkward to walk into the wind.
8	34–40 knots	**Gale:** moderately high waves with edges that break into spindrift or heavy foam; branches begin to break from the trees and it becomes genuinely hard to walk anywhere because of the wind.
9	41–47 knots	**Strong gale:** high waves, foam so dense that it begins to make it difficult to see properly; expect to lose slates and the odd chimney pot.
10	48–55 knots	**Storm:** very high waves, foam blows even further, making visibility even worse; trees may uproot, and the wind causes minor structural damage.
11	56–63 knots	**Violent storm:** the waves are now exceptionally high—high enough to conceal a medium-sized ship—and entire areas may appear white; visibility is even more reduced; on land, expect widespread structural damage.

Lightning Storms

Hmm, this doesn't look good. You're on the water, one of the best conductors of electricity, and the mast of your boat is pointing up into the atmosphere like a built-in lightning rod. What can you do to minimize the damage if lightning strikes? If you can, turn off your electronic systems and remove the battery cables; consider having a spare hand-held VHF radio that you can carry around with you so you can turn the main one off. Have the grounding system on the boat checked periodically to make sure that there's no problem with arcing. There's no right or wrong way to make a good radio-frequency ground on a boat—some use an area of copper foil, others argue that a leaded keel is the best solution—but if you go out regularly in an environment where storms are an issue, you need to seek advice.

Receiving Weather Forecasts

Although you should already have a good idea of what the weather's got planned for you before you cast off, you'll also need to keep up to speed with what's going on. So, having checked the TV, Internet, and the harbor or marina master's wall for the latest information, what else do you have at your disposal? Although it's possible to receive weather updates via SMS on a cell phone, you can't rely on it. Instead, use your VHF radio. Some have built-in weather channels, but if yours doesn't you need to check the sources and frequencies of the broadcasts you should be listening to: specifically the weather forecasts and the Coast Guard or equivalent (usually channel 16). Although VHF only has a limit of between 5 and 25 miles—VHF radios communicate by line of sight, so it depends on the conditions, the physical geography, and so on— it is monitored 24 hours a day, so is always your best way of getting help.

Force 2: light breeze

Force 5: a fresh breeze with moderate waves

Force 8: a gale is blowing and the sea shows plenty of white tops

Force 10: storm conditions with high waves and foam blowing

Distress Signals

In the unlikely event that it all goes horribly wrong and you need to be able to attract attention to your plight, then there is a range of devices and techniques available to get you noticed. In some situations, this will be as simple as hailing a fellow canal-boat owner as they saunter by, or waving at the guy in the canoe on the other side of the river, but sometimes circumstances will dictate otherwise, and you need to be prepared.

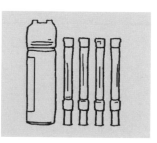

Flares

Flares come packed in waterproof containers with instructions on the side. It's generally good practice to replace unused ones after four years. There are basically three types of flare that can be used in an emergency to attract attention. These are:

• Hand-Held Flares

These come in white, red, and orange, and are useful for different situations.

White flares are typically very bright, and are used to show the position of your boat if you fear a collision is about to occur—for example, if you're drifting in the dark. Red flares can be seen much further away— up to 3 miles—and burn for about a minute. Orange smoke flares are used when visibility is good; they burn brightly, giving off heaps of smoke, but only for about 10 seconds.

• Airborne Flares

These are used to attract attention when help is a long way away. For example, parachute rockets shoot up to about 1,000 ft and then burn for around 40 seconds; they can be seen up to 25 miles away in good, clear weather. Alternatively, aerial red meteors are fired from a pistol or a special launcher.

• Buoyant Orange Smoke

A variant of the hand-held version—dropped into the water it burns for about three minutes; normally used to signal your position to air rescue services.

What if I Don't Have Anything with Me?

If you've been foolish enough to come out without any means of attracting attention, then there's still an internationally recognized cry for help. Stand—very carefully—and face the direction that you expect help to come from; then stretch your arms out on either side to make a T-shape. Slowly raise and lower your arms, keeping them outstretched.

Flare Safety and Use

A misfired flare can easily add to your problems rather than coming to your rescue. Flares can start a fire on the boat, particularly in the sails, or set trees alight if you're firing them from a remote shore where you've had to land. The best thing to do is to treat them like firearms—keep them safe and study how to use them properly. Store them in a watertight container, make sure you know where they are, don't point them at anyone, hold them away from your body, and let them off downwind.

Note: Flares should only be used in an emergency. They are not fireworks, and letting them off is not "a bit of fun". A flare tells other sailors and the emergency services that you are in trouble; in some regions, letting them off when you are not in distress is an offence.

Flags

Flags have advantages and disadvantages compared with flares. They are less visible over a long distance, but they don't "run out". The standard distress flag is made of orange plastic and has a black square with a black circle flying over it; it's typically about 3x3 ft. Another flag that you'll see from time to time has an orange "X" against a white background; this means that the person requires help, but is not a distress signal. Alternatively, if you've got the flag of your country on board, you can theoretically fly this upside down as a distress signal—though this is problematic with some national flags which aren't enormously different when flown upside down and viewed from a distance, or when visibility is poor.

Other Methods

There are various other ways to attract attention should you get into difficulties, including:

- A non-pyrotechnic device for use at night—this is typically an auto-SOS light which, when you switch it on, flashes the dot–dash pattern for SOS automatically. Obviously, it's important to make sure that the batteries are working before every trip and to carry spares in case they aren't.
- A simple mirror is an amazingly effective signaling device in clear conditions with good sunshine; it's obviously less effective in other circumstances. Hold it by the edges, and aim it in the direction from which you think rescue might be coming, rocking the mirror up and down to produce a regular flash. In perfect conditions, pilots have reported seeing a signal mirror flashing almost 100 miles away.

- A foghorn—the modern version can be used to create a series of uniformly long blasts to attract attention.
- If you regularly spend time on the ocean or on very large lakes, then consider an EPIRB—an emergency position-indicating radio beacon—which will beam your position to rescue services. Some sailors also carry PLBs—personal locator beacons—which do the same job.

Glossary of Terms

Like most specialist activities, boating has generated an extraordinary amount of jargon, much of it specifically to do with sailboats. In this glossary we'll be picking up a few sailing terms, but we've tried to concentrate on those words that occur no matter what kind of boating you're interested in. As we've said elsewhere, this book is the paper equivalent of an afternoon on the water—a taster, to see if you like the view, the weather, and the overall experience.

Abeam at right angles to the keel (i.e. the center line) of the boat.

Aft towards the back end of the boat (the stern).

Ahead in front of the boat, or in a forward direction.

Aids to navigation man-made devices—such as buoys—used variously to indicate safe passage, or potential dangers.

Backfire flame control a device on the carburetor of a boat designed to stop the ignition of gasoline vapors in the event of an engine backfire.

Beam the widest part of the boat.

Beaufort scale the system invented by Sir Francis Beaufort in 1805 to measure wind strength.

Berth a location in a port where a boat can be moored; also, a place to sleep (usually a bunk) on a boat.

Bilge an area at the bottom of some boats where water that can't run off the decks collects; this has to be periodically pumped dry.

Buoy a man-made floating marker.

Canal boat a long boat, typically 60ft, designed for cruising slowly down inland canals; many are luxurious enough to live on permanently (houseboats).

Canoe a small, narrow boat, typically for one or two people, powered by oars and usually, but not always, open on top.

Catamaran a boat with two hulls, joined in the middle by a frame.

Cleat an anvil-shaped fixing point on a boat or dock, around which a rope can be looped or lashed.

Daggerboard a keel which slides in a casing and can be pulled up or pushed down.

Dead reckoning a way of plotting a course without instruments by extrapolating from your last known position.

Dinghy either a small "utility" craft like a rowboat that's carried by a larger vessel, or a small sailboat, often used for racing.

Draft the distance from the surface of the water to the lowest point of the boat (the tip of the keel).

Drysuit a one-piece suit, sealed at the wrists, ankles, and neck; designed to prevent water from entering at all.

Fenders devices that hang at the side of a boat and are designed to absorb the shock when you bump into something else, such as a dock or another boat.

Freeboard the distance between the surface of the water and the upper deck level, usually measured at the center of the boat.

Galley the kitchen on board a boat.

Give-way vessel the vessel which is required to take evasive action when two boats approach each other and are in danger of colliding.

GPS (Global Positioning System) a network of satellites orbiting the earth which can be "pinged" by a device on board a boat to find out its exact location.

Gunwale the top edge of the side of a boat.

Head a boat's toilet.

Hull the body of the boat. A displacement hull plows through the water; a planing hull skims across its surface.

Inflatable any kind of boat that can be blown up and then deflated for easier storage and transportation (see RIB).

Kayak a boat that shares many of the characteristics of a canoe, but which is usually covered at the top, rather than open.

Keel the boat's central "fin," which is weighted (usually with lead) and extends down into the water to help stop the boat from tipping over.

Latitude the location of a place in terms of its position north or south of the equator.

Leeward away from the wind; also downwind.

Lock a device on a waterway that allows the water level to be raised or lowered so that boats can move from one level to another.

Longitude the location of a place to the east or west of the meridian at Greenwich, which is at 0° longitude.

Marina a harbor with shops, fuel, and leisure facilities.

Marine Survey an inspection by a professional surveyor, required when applying for insurance for a boat.

MARPOL trash placard a sign indicating that a boat follows the internationally recognized standards for disposing of waste; MARPOL stands for "MARine POLlution."

MMSI (Maritime Mobile Service Identity) a unique number that is transmitted automatically alongside every radio message and can be used to identify an individual boat.

Mooring any place where a boat can be tied up.

Narrowboat a British term for a canal boat.

Personal watercraft a jet ski or similar.

PFD (personal flotation device) a flotation aid such as a life jacket, or a lifebelt thrown to people in the water.

Port the left side of the boat when you're facing forward.

RIB (rigid inflatable boat) a boat in which only part of the hull is inflatable.

Semaphore a system of spelling out words using flags.

Sextant a device used to navigate by the positions of the sun, moon, and stars.

Slip or slipway an inclined ramp used for getting boats into and out of the water.

Stand-on vessel the vessel which has right of way when two vessels are approaching one another.

Starboard the right side of the boat when you're facing forward.

Stern the back of the boat.

Tiller the lever which is used to steer a boat by controlling the rudder.

VHF (very high frequency) radio radio system used by boats for communicating with each other, with the Coast Guard, receiving weather forecasts, etc.

Wetsuit a one-piece suit of neoprene that traps a thin layer of water next to the skin, where it is then heated by the body.

Windward towards the wind; the side of the boat nearest the wind.

Supplies and Equipment

West Marine
Boating equipment, gear, and apparel.
Tel: 1-800-685-4838; www.westmarine.com

BoatnDock
Supplies for boathouses and docks.
www.boatndock.com

Owners' Information and Associations

BoatU.S.
Information about insurance, storage, local regulations, and safety tips.
Boat Owner's Association of the United States
880 South Pickett Street, Alexandria, VA 22304; Tel: 1-800-395-2628; www.boatus.com

Discover Boating
Public awareness effort managed by the National Marine Manufacturers Association
(NMMA). Resources and frequently asked questions about owning a boat.
National Marine Manufacturers Association
200 E. Randolph Dr. Suite 5100, Chicago, IL 60601; Tel: (312) 946-6200;
www.discoverboating.com

Association of Marina Industries
Nonprofit concerning the marina industry.
AMI, 444 North Capitol St. NW, Suite 645, Washington, DC 20001; Tel: (202) 737-9775;
www.marinaassociation.org

Weather and Safety

U.S. Coast Guard Office of Boating Safety
National boating regulations and information about safe boating.
www.uscgboating.org

National Oceanic and Atmospheric Administrations's National Weather Service
Watercraft-related information on oceanic and atmospheric conditions.
www.nws.noaa.gov

Environmental Organizations

Recreational Boating and Fishing Foundation
Increases interest in recreational angling and raises awareness of aquatic conservation.
www.rbff.org

Ocean Conservancy
Restores fisheries, protects wildlife, conserves ecosystems, and encourages better
stewardship. 2029 K Street, NW, Washington, DC 20006; Tel: 1-800-519-1541;
www.oceanconservancy.org